AGAVE

AGAVE

A Celebration of Tequila
in Story, Song, Poetry, Essay,
and Graphic Art

Edited by
Ashley and Nathan Brown

INK
BRUSH
PRESS

ISBN: 978-0-9839715-1-1
Library of Congress Control Number: 2011940932

Book Design by Ashley and Nathan Brown
Front Cover Art: Norma Brown
Back Cover Photograph: Terry Dalrymple

Ink Brush Press
Temple and Dallas, Texas
www.inkbrushpress.com

We dedicate this book to our favorite bartenders:

Renée, Lorelee, James, and Kellie

CONTENTS

Introduction: What Brings Us to the Table, Ashley Brown
xiii

Our Three Favorite Margaritas in Our Favorite Towns,
Ashley and Nathan Brown
1

El Gusano Rojo: The Worm, Sherry Craven
5

Body Shots, Patrick Ocampo
6

There Is No Worm, Patrick Ocampo
7

Another Shot of Añejo, Gretchen Harries Graham
9

Mayahuel, Larry D. Thomas
11

A Parrot Head's Wasted Thoughts, Alan Berecka
12

Agave Cactus, Carol Hamilton
13

Tequila Nostalgia, Lise Liddell
14

Con Gusano, Anne McCrady
20

Margarita, Jerry Bradley
21

Your Margaritas, David Rains
23

order, Milton Brasher-Cunningham
27

How to Make a Long Island Iced Tea, Millard Dunn
28

Dias de Las Margaritas, Karla K. Morton
29

Before Goodbye, David Meischen
31

Tequila's Accomplice, Kellie Salome
32

Their Fourth Ph.D. Discuss Party, James Ragan
35
José Cuervo, Cindy Jordan
36
Grace, Beth Robinson
38
Good Tequila, Naked Women, and Blue Bell Ice Cream,
Terry Dalrymple
39
Tex in Ten, Laurence Musgrove
45
Tequila Talk, James Hoggard
46
Blue Margaritas, Carol Hamilton
47
Tequila Dragons, Steven Schroeder, Yang Qian,
and Mary Ann O'Donnell
48
Write about Tequila, Hannah Rappaport
52
McAllen, Room 263, Juan Manuel Perez
54
Sonoran Monsoon Season, Audell Shelburne
55
Tequila Chicken, Barrie Scardino
57
Two Dogs Howling at the Moon, David Parsons
59
Five Acres North of the Red River, Jim Spurr
61
Lips Like Pink Elephants, Andrew Geyer
62
I stared hard..., Tony Mares
69
Fifth Symphony, Gary Hawkins
71
What I Learned from the Fugitive's Mother, Robert Ashker Kraft
72
Bacardi Margarita, Antonia Murguia
77

Diving into Love, Jerry Bradley
78
Five Easy Margaritas, Sherry Craven
79
Old Man, Robert Whitsitt
80
The Second One, Sandra Soli
97
La Señorita Margarita, Scott Wiggerman
98
Redbird, Tequila and Me, Cindy Jordan
99
Norte Americanos, R. Dean Johnson
100
Tequila Sunrise, Julie Chappell
109
A Little Rain in Arkansas, George Wallace
111
Tequila Brings Peace to Mideast, Jeffrey DeLotto
112
El Patrón, Karla K. Morton
114
Christmas Proof, A. William Hinson
116
The Tab, Lyman Grant
117
A Day in the Life of an Insurance Adjuster, Jim Spurr
120
all my doors are open, Steven Schroeder
121
The Number You Have Reached, Melvin Sterne
123
Love Poem, Robert Wynne
131
Dual Dominance, Joyce Gullickson
132
Tasty Tequila Teacakes, Barrie Scardino
133
Parallax View, Jim McGarrah
136

Uncovering the Mystery of Mezcal, Michele Ostrove
137
Margarita Pie, Norma Brown
139
The Middle Name of Evil, Alan Birkelbach
140
Apply Imagination, Carol Hamilton
145
Tequila Nonsense, W.K. Stratton
146
Down, Nathan Brown
147
Contributors
149

GRAPHIC ART BY

Christine Russell
8
Daniella DeLaRue
19
Nathan Brown
22
Christine Russell
30
Laurence Musgrove
45
Mary Ann O'Donnell
51
Audell Shelburne
56
Christine Russell
70
Terry Dalrymple
83
Terry Dalrymple
96
Norma Brown
110
Ebbesen Davis
115
Lisa Craig
119
Christine Russell
135

Introduction: What Brings Us to the Table

When Nathan and I were introduced on a February afternoon at the 2007 Folk Alliance Conference in Memphis, the first question out of his mouth—after I told him I was from Houston—was, "Where would somebody get the best margarita in that big town?" That evening, we met up for margaritas in the Marriott lobby bar, both relieved to have found a drinking buddy. The bartender served our two $11 margaritas in Styrofoam cups; they had run out of clean glasses. He had kindly tried to salt the rims, but the Styrofoam wasn't really holding the salt. Nathan and I toasted...to great margaritas...even if those were two of the worst we'd ever had.

Months later, when he passed through Houston on his way to Greece, we met for margaritas and *queso fundido* at Teala's. Much better than the Marriott. Things were looking up. We toasted to great margaritas again, and to a new friendship.

Months after that "date," I went to Austin to see my best friend and some good live music. Nathan happened to be in Wimberley, so he joined me and Sarah at our favorite semi-upscale Mexican restaurant in town, Manuel's...where the three of us spent hours talking and laughing while the waiter supplied us with a constant flow of happy hour appetizers, House Ritas, and other tequila-based drinks with names like Pink Chihuahua and Sunburn.

Finally, in August, we met for the fourth time...in Austin, just the two of us. I made blue margaritas. Since then, I have relocated to Oklahoma; we've gotten married; and, in addition to shaping our life together, it has become a shared mission to search for the best margaritas in the Southwest and to talk (more than we ought to perhaps) about our findings with friends and other fellow margarita lovers. This might be why Ink Brush Press approached us with the idea for this book. And when we put out the call for submissions, we quickly discovered that many people share our passion. As a compliment to all of their contributions, we wanted to include, here at the beginning, the results—up to this point—of our research. It's been hard work, but somebody's got to do it.

Ashley Brown

Our Three Favorite Margaritas in Our Favorite Towns
Ashley and Nathan Brown

With our deep mutual appreciation for those few spots that actually make a better margarita than we can shake at home, we've ended up with quite a list of drinks and places—each with a unique characteristic that earned the margarita its place on our list of favorites. Enjoy!

Houston

Hugo's Gran Reposado

Hugo's — *Gran Reposado* — Hugo's treats margaritas with the utmost respect. When the head chef is in charge of the recipes, you know something's up. They have an impressive list of top-shelf tequilas. They do not serve frozen margaritas, as this would be an insult to the tequila. Their all-around best rita is the $10 Gran Reposado, made with Hussong Reposado, Gran Marnier, lemon and lime juice; we also love the unique Oaxacan made with smoky Monte Alban Mezcal instead of tequila.

El Patio—*Blue Margarita*—This makes the list, not necessarily because it is consistently tasty and well-made, but because it's probably the strongest margarita in Texas, if not the Western Hemisphere. Rumor is that, in addition to the usual ingredients, they pour in a dash of Everclear. You may forget the hours that follow the downing of this margarita, but if you pass through Houston, it's something you just ought to try (if you have a designated driver lined up).

Under the Volcano—*House Margarita*—This tropical paradise, which serves as an everyday celebration of the Day of the Dead (as well as Malcolm Lowry's novel *Under the Volcano*), is the best place in Houston,

Manuel's House Rita

in our opinion, to enjoy a Happy Hour margarita. The bartenders make only high quality drinks with tremendous care and the freshest of ingredients. A warning: if you end up on the patio—with the greenery hiding the busy Houston streets, the jukebox playing tunes from the best selection of music in town, the fans whirring away—with a margarita or two or three, you may find yourself losing hours of your afternoon while you forget all sense of responsibility, things to do, and places to go.

Austin

Manuel's—*Happy Hour House Rita*—For a mere $4, this is the best deal in the Southwest. Not only can you get a great, relatively strong house rita, they also offer half-price appetizers daily during Happy Hour. This is —without a doubt—our favorite spot to go before a night out in Austin to meet friends, or to simply revel in the wonderful, tasty goodness of it all.

Continental Club — *Kellie-rita* (not the 'official' name)—If you like your margaritas tart enough to make you suck your lips back into your throat and out your ears, then head on over to the Continental on a Wednesday night (when you'll have the best chance to hear Jon Dee

2

Graham and James McMurtry both) and talk to Kellie, bartendress extraordinaire. Ask her for that high maintenance margarita that she makes for that damned poet Nathan Brown when he comes to town and bugs her while she should be working. If you're nice, and tip well, she might make it for you. By the way, Kellie contributed the fabulous piece, "Tequila's Accomplice," to this anthology.

Matt's El Rancho—*Janie's Margarita* or *The TKO Martini*—When so many places have a notable "not-rightness" about them—and especially their margaritas—Matt's just seems to have some kind of "rightness" about it. It is a wonderful, long-standing family restaurant on South Lamar in Austin, and the bar is relaxed (except during the busy hours of the evening meal, and especially on weekends). You can get some great appetizers. And the bartenders are usually nice when it comes to conversation about *tequilas y margaritas*.

Santa Fe and Taos

Inn of the Anasazi's Silver Coin

Inn of the Anasazi—*Silver Coin* and *Ultima Gold*—Simply put, we consider the Silver Coin and Ultima Gold at the beautiful little bar in the Inn of the Anasazi to be, quite possibly, the best margaritas anywhere. Don't look at the price. Just order them. We recommend one of each in order to compare and contrast. Just off the plaza in Santa Fe, it's also one of the most quiet, charming, and romantic locations to enjoy a margarita and some excellent bar food.

Doc Martin's (Taos Inn)—*Cowboy Buddha*—While we've also experimented with the Horny Toad and Baby Buddha (not sure why we ever chose a baby-sized margarita), Doc Martin's Cowboy Buddha—paired with their Chile Relleno—has been known to inspire us to drive from Santa Fe to Taos for no other reason than to sip on this salty, limey mixture of Herradura Silver, Cointreau, and hand-squeezed lime juice, while gazing out the window onto Paseo del Pueblo Norte, feeling the warm buzziness of the altitude and good tequila combined.

Maria's—*House Margarita*—When we need a break from the generally exorbitant menu prices found at the lovely restaurants on and near Santa Fe's plaza, we head over to Maria's on Cordova Road where they have a reasonably-priced menu of consistently tasty New-Mexican standards—and the largest margarita menu we've ever seen, all made with the finest ingredients, including fresh-squeezed lemon juice (as lemons yield more juice year-round). You might get distracted by the more gourmet, and astonishingly pricey, La Margarita de Paradiso or El Baile del Sol (that boasts of being Robert Redford's favorite), but we recommend the good ole house margarita as by far the most affordable, yet satisfying, margarita in Santa Fe.

El Gusano Rojo: The Worm
Sherry Craven

Ah, beautiful blue agave reaching your strong arms
up into the Jalisco skies, digging your soul into
the volcanic soil settling into shiny obsidian,

harboring the *gusano rojo* just for my bottle
of mezcal, the proud parent of tequila.

Gracias para su regalo, the gift of spirits,
from the spirits, giving me mystical visions
into the meaning of life or maybe love even.

Gracias. Your descendants, mezcal and tequila,
and earlier, pulque, sweet, smoldering, and cloudy, potent
enough to ferment my thoughts before I throw

myself from the cliff of too much reason. *Gracias*.
For 1000 years pulque simmered in the Mexican sun,
fizzed in the Mexican mouth, and gave birth to mezcal wine

and now the grandchild, tequila, with or without *el gusano rojo*
in the bottom of the bottle, a larvae full of protein and firewater.
Yo le doy mil gracias, many thanks for the three million

blue agave yuccas growing in Jalisco that will end up as pure
silver sun in my chilled stemmed glass tonight. *Mil gracias*.

Body Shots
Patrick Ocampo

You will remember the tarantula sting of her, the sweet citrus of her lime soaked lips, and the knockout punch of her smile. You will remember the taste of her salt, the curve of her neck, the puckering sweetness of her scent, the blue agave of her eyes. This is the spontaneous intimacy of a stranger's body, the uncertainty of thought, the calypso beating of the heart, the sunburst of her hair as it brushes your face. There is a hint of daring, a challenge in what she is offering, as if she is testing how far you will go at the first encounter. She is moving now, her shoulder sliding, pouring another round into you. The silver liquidity slides down your throat and instills your veins with warmth, igniting a fire in you as bright as a desert mirage. There is pain, a throbbing in your mind that you will regret this; that you will regret her, but she intoxicates you as she traces lines across her skin for your tongue to follow. You are spiraling now, repeating the motions, salt, silver, citrus, forgetting your reasons and your limits, while she is dropping you to the floor with each careful shot to the body.

There Is No Worm
Patrick Ocampo

"There is no worm"
she tells me,
after the first glass
"it's only a myth,
something
they made up
for the tourists."
I am trying
to focus
on her
but her freckles
and flaming hair
contrast so brilliantly
with the lime
and ice.
She is blasting
the truth
through me
with every shot,
shattering
the fakery
of my vacation
from myself.
I am not
the man
behind the shades,
and she knows it.
I wish I could
extinguish her,
to keep her
in the dark
but she is too bright
and like
the worm
that doesn't exist,
she is impossible
to swallow.

Christine Russell

Another Shot of Añejo
Gretchen Harries Graham

There was that first tequila night, not that different from the other
    voices you've heard.
And everyone swore the stuff off forever.
The super model who dated one of our best friends was in town from
    Paris.
She didn't eat food, but by God she drank tequila, and wore handmade
    Italian cowboy boots.
We drank. It was yellow. The night was as long as a sickened sailor's
    first ride on the high seas.
That was before I knew Añejo.

Ten years down the line, on a late, hot August afternoon, a dashing
    Spaniard from Juarez,
introduced me to Añejo.
We had just come from a swim in the wondrous, cooling waters of
    Barton Springs.
The Spaniard offered, "You must drink the nectar of my people."
After a couple rounds, I was pretty sure it could fuel us all night long
    and we'd be in Puerto
Escondido by the next day, surfing the sun as it sank off the Emerald
    Coast, drinking Añejo until we
had lived about as large as we could have ever possibly dreamed. That's
    just how good it tasted, one after
Another shot of Añejo.

Añejo can usher you across the line whether you are prim and proper,
    or straight up vampish.
Añejo makes everyone a Latin lover.
It will get you closer to a lover's touch than you've ever been, and offer
    you laughter at the same time.
If the future has a past, lately mine can be told with a pale agave liquid
    poured over ice with fresh squeezed limes, thank you very much.
If you drink enough of the smooth, sensual, sultry spirit, it can make the
    distance between you and another melt within a few shots.
You will fly, clothes strewn, phones ringing, people wondering where

the hell you are.

A 15- minute parking time zone turns into lost tequila hours, gasping
    for air from torrid kisses and

Another shot of Añejo.

I prefer to be a longed for valentine, embraced while sipping tequila all
    night long.

I was once enchanted with being someone's wife.

Then my husband went to war, a war as big as World War II.

Words get blown up in planes being shot down over Japan and the
    Saharan Desert.

If you love an addict, it leaves a brown spot on your heart.

It's not possible to find definition as time slips away and the Cimmerian
    shade falls.

As they wield out of control, light returns with

Another shot of Añejo.

There are some places in Mexico where people savor Añejo all day long.

Some sip it to make them numb, others to make them strong.

Some days I do too.

The rains came but they didn't wash us clean.

At the end of the season all that was left to do was

ship him off to heal the wounds that he had won in battle.

The path is turning under our feet.

In a November slip, as the sun sets, I watch the Austin sky turn pink,

and feel the open smile and warmth of

Another shot of Añejo.

Mayahuel (Aztec Goddess of Fertility and Agave)
Larry D. Thomas

Her demon grandmother,
Tzitzimitl, gorged light
and blanketed Mother Earth
with palpable darkness.

Dispatched by Tzitzimitl
to execute her for fleeing
the heavens with Quetzalcoatl,
the demon stars bared

their gleaming, slimy teeth,
and devoured her. Down to her bones,
the demon stars feasted.
From her buried, gnawed remains

sprouted the blue
agave, charred by lightning
to nothing but its heart
whose sacred nectar

fermented, nourishing
the light-starved natives
with the holy glow
of pulque, tequila.

A Parrot Head's Wasted Thoughts

Alan Berecka

Geourgi a Bulgarian legend told me
he writes poetry because he knows
it is necessary. I know a poet
from Oklahoma who carries a flask
of tequila. He says he needs it
because bars often screw with the ratio
of booze and juice in his favorite drink.

I once heard that Rita Hayworth, actress
and pin-up model, inspired the Margarita
which is served in a glass that some
say is a mutant form of the champagne coup—
a glass that I heard was modeled, molded
really, on the breast of Marie Antoinette.

I had an uncle who said he had to drive
because he was too drunk to walk, and I
am driven to wonder if Rita Hayworth's
breasts were ever rimmed with salt,
or how large the poet's flask would be
if glass blowers and barkeeps had waited
to be inspired by Annette Funicello.

Agave Cactus

Carol Hamilton

You don't squeeze tequila
from a pumped up, rubbery leaf.
Nothing is easy in Mexico,
and everything takes time,
patience, muscle. Hacking
and digging and hacking
and a deep pit and fire
and time and time and time.
I lose time, forget it at
the other end of the tequila,
but left to me, that cactus
would still be standing there
on the Sonora Desert
                    undisturbed.

Tequila Nostalgia
Lise Liddell

My greatest tequila memory—and considering how much of it I drank I am surprised I have any recollection of it at all—spawned itself when my brother was a sophomore and I was a junior at The University of Texas at Austin in the late spring of 1984. The two of us and Frank's girlfriend, Carlene, decided to take a routine road trip to Mexico, as college students are prone to embark upon random adventures that require time, energy, and money they don't have, just to see what kind of fun time lies waiting out beyond the campus horizon.

In the early 80's, hauling your butt down to Mexico with your college chums stuffed in your Cutlass Calais, with its sunroof busted and stuck open, was not the scary prospect it is today. You needed nothing to cross the border except maybe a driver's license for whomever was the designated driver—which back then was not someone abstaining from alcohol; it was just someone who owned, or whose parents owned, the car. Whole busses of frat boys would go to Boys Town to lose their virginity. They might come back having lost all their money, too, but losing their lives to the random spray of bullets by a drug cartel was never a concern.

The legal drinking age in Texas at the time was 18 and "carding" was almost non-existent. I believe at that time the drinking age in Mexico was maybe 2, if there was one at all. People drove drunk all over Texas and Mexico. There were hardly any cars on the road back then. You were a lot more likely to hit an armadillo than another vehicle. During my childhood in Houston, my own parents drove drunk countless times, with their three kids tossed in the back of the station wagon doing summer-saults and having fist fights. No seat belts, as there were no seat belt laws. And if we had to drive more than two hours, mom and dad plunked down a cooler stocked with Carta Blanca beer on the front seat between the two of them, chugged down one beer after another, and then tossed the bottles out the window. This was also before the onset of "Don't Mess with Texas."

Therefore, driving your naïve drunken ass down to Mexico, all over the tarnation of Mexico, and then back into the heart of Texas was only a cause for jubilation, and absolutely no cause for concern in 1984. You could even tell your parents about a trip like that, and the only response would be something to the effect that if you had that much time to goof off you'd better be making decent grades. So we trucked it to Mexico frequently, usually heading to Laredo where a high percentage of the UT student body could be found on any given day.

On this trip, however, we decided to go to Piedras Negras, right across the border from Eagle Pass where Frank had been on a few hunting trips. The day was a beautiful bright spring day that was already feeling like summer at around 85 degrees, and the three of us were high on college-aged adrenalin and idiocy. We whizzed down I-35 South to San Antonio, jumped onto US-57 South, and exuberantly hi-fived and cheered at several Mexican Federales as we crossed the Mexican border about four hours after takeoff. We headed straight to Club Moderno, where Frank had been informed by a reliable frat-brother source that the owner had invented the Nacho. As far as I'm concerned, the nacho is a far more enlightened invention than boring old sliced bread. The three of us were headed for Mexican Mecca.

At about two in the afternoon, we walked underneath the standard neon signs that decorate all Mexican restaurants into a boxed building with not a single window. Apparently the lack of natural light, and however much money he'd made on the Nacho copyright, was no inspiration to the King of Nachos to install lighting fixtures in his restaurant. The inside was lit with 25-watt light bulbs crammed into some kind of wacky wire fixtures posing as chandeliers hanging from the ceiling, and a few blood-red glass votives glowing on each table. The room was as good as pitch black. The place had about 20 four-top wooden tables with dilapidated wooden chairs scattered about. Only a few tables were occupied with what looked to be like Mexican businessmen smoking fat cigarettes and fatter cigars, and getting plowed on various tequila drinks.

We sat down and ordered a round of margaritas, along with a plate of truly original nachos. The nachos were definitely worth making the trip for—made with light crispy fried flour tortillas, a tender blanket of melted cheddar cheese over homemade spicy borracho beans, and slices of fresh jalapeno heaped on top; they were truly divine. I hate to admit it about my own beloved state, but back then the standard Texas nacho usually involved pre-packaged stale corn tortilla chips, 2 lb cans of beans, and 1 lb blocks of Velveeta "cheese."

And let's get to the real delicacy: those Mexican jalapeños were not the rubbery things you get in a jar in the U.S. that taste more like bad pickles, and not the hybrid fresh ones that are so mild you could put them in baby food. These bastards were the real deal—strong enough to immediately trigger the onset of dehydration through overproduction of fluid through your sweat glands, requiring of course the emergency mass consumption of...tequila infused beverages!

And speaking of, the margaritas were better than any I'd ever had in all my young years of Texas living and drinking. There are no margarita "mixes" in Mexico, and none of that frozen goo that comes pooping out of a machine. Mexican margaritas are made with 100% freshly squeezed lime juice from the most excellent limes on the planet. A Mexican lime is no bigger than a Texas pecan, but it holds about six times as much juice as most larger American limes, and about two times as much as a Florida Key lime. The flavor is tart, tangy, but not acidic. You can drink your fill of margaritas without getting that nasty stomach burn. Then of course there is the tequila, akin to the champagne of France, as it is made only in Mexico, and the Mexicans know how the hell to manhandle their homegrown spirit. Our drinks were most likely made with Sauza or José Cuervo, two of the oldest and most prominent tequila makers in Mexico, a little Cointreau, and of course the lime juice. We sucked 'em down like Slurpies.

After another two rounds, a bowl of guacamole, and a mess of enchiladas, the waiter suggested we try a Tequila Sour, made with tequila, a little lemon juice and sugar. We "hell-yeah!" 'ed him, and started into tequila course number two, drink number four of the afternoon.

About this time two friendly Mexican Mariachis, resting their gut string guitars on top of their jolly lard shelves, showed up to serenade the crowd. Since we were 50% of the crowd and the only ones getting riled up and making noise, the guitarists planted themselves next to our table and began to sing, upon my request, "La Cucaracha" (The Roach, in Spanish), a song I had long cherished since first hearing it in elementary school. We gave the performers a huge round of drunken applause and then quickly secured a first name basis with them, giving them each of our nicknames: Fish for Frank, Chopper for Carlene, and Diesel for me. Before long we had gotten chummy enough with the guys that they pulled up chairs, and Chopper—being a gracious hostess— ordered each of them a tequila sour. The three of us joined in the music fest—singing songs we didn't know, in a language we didn't know. Tequila has a way of granting its worshippers spontaneous knowledge.

After a while, Fish asked the boys if he could play one of their guitars. A guitar was happily handed to him as the two singers discovered a potential brother in music. Fish played Neil Young's "Needle and the Damage Done," then The Grateful Dead's "Death Don't Have No Mercy," and finally, Elton John's "Goodbye Yellow Brick Road." Each of us sang these depressing anthems like we were at a UT football game belting out fight songs. We had some more tequila sours, and after about an hour of passionate camaraderie between folks of different cultures and countries, the players announced they needed to move on to other tables, as new patrons were arriving, and then asked Fish to hand over the "beinte dollares" he owed them for guitar rental. The three of us were a bit startled that our new best friends actually wanted money from us. Frank somehow bargained the guys down to ten bucks, while Carlene and I scrounged around in our pockets and purses for cash. We paid the boys, took their request for money as a sign from God that it was time to get the hell outta dodge, paid the bill, and headed for the exit.

We stumbled our way out of the cool dark comfort of our cave into the cruel scalding Mexican sunlight, which, coupled with the astounding amount of tequila boiling in our brains and guts, caused the immediate stopping of our feet in their tracks, intense pupil dilation, and throbbing migraine pangs that we felt had been inflicted upon us by pure evil.

We were hosed.

Each of us planted a hand over our eyes and cursed the sun god with an astounding plethora of expletives in both English and Spanish. With one small step for the college buffoons that we were, we went from feeling like we were approaching spiritual revelation with our kindred Mexican brothers to knowing decidedly that we had been plunged into the ninth ring of hell with Satan himself getting ready to feast on our tequila-saturated limbs and organs.

We staggered to the car for what we felt sure was going to be the eternal drive home, and serendipitously ran into a nasty traffic jam trying to cross the border. We were literally stopped still in the middle of the street for 45 minutes, the three of us sitting in the car sweating and bitching about the torture we were being subjected to and how we never should have thought up this ridiculous scheme in the first place, when Fish looked over and noticed a market with cases of beer stacked in front of it. He jumped out of the car, ran in, and bought two cases of miniature Corona beers. Chopper hopped into the back seat with him and they popped beers for each of us, saving us from the pain of sobering up in 90-degree weather with an A/C not equipped to duke it out with a car sitting in idle with a permanently open sunroof.

I began to play chauffer and DJ, and we quickly got on our happy role again singing along to the 120-minute Jimmy Buffett cassette tape I'd made by recording two of his "ode to fun" LPs onto one tape. We were definitely "wasted away, again in Margaritaville." There were plenty of "fins to the left, and fins to the right," that looked a lot like Mexicans. We didn't "know where we were gonna go when the volcano blew," but we didn't care as long as there was plenty of tequila there. Finally, we told ourselves that "come Monday it'll be alright," as long as we made it back to school and sobered up in time for Fish to take his "History of Mexico" test, and for all of us to attend our disgustingly sober respective sorority and fraternity meetings. But for now, the tequila was good and still taking care of us, with a bit of nurturing from little brother Corona.

It took us about six hours to get back to Austin. By that time the tequila had simmered way down, and the miniature Coronas had worn out their piggyback ride.

Obviously, the only thing to do was to drive directly to Jorge's Mexican Restaurant and order margaritas. Not as tasty as the real deal in Piedras, Negras, but a perfect ending to one of the most memorable days of my life. Chopper and Fish ended up marrying different people, but the three of us remain close friends, and of course each of us remains quite fond of tequila. When I told Fish I was writing a story about this, he said that recently he'd talked to a Mexican friend of his and asked him if he'd been to Piedras Negras lately. His buddy replied, "No way, Amigo. The shitiest, meanest people migrate to that city." Still, part of Diesel believes I'd jump into my 12 year old Jeep Cherokee with its very own busted sunroof to meet Chopper, Fish, and José Cuervo at Club Moderno, any time, any day, in a heartbeat.

Daniella DeLaRue

Con Gusano
Anne McCrady

Para todo mal, mezcal y para todo bien también.
—Oaxacan proverb

Visiting Mexico, the heart of their marriage
grown hard as the volcanic gravel underfoot,
they search for healing *en las montañas.*
The landscape, no salve for their misery;
the conversation stings and bites.
Like a cruel tour guide, he walks her weaknesses,
as she looks beyond him for what they have lost.
Stumbling over words sharp as cactus,
among *los campos de agave*, they count regrets
that are endless as the rows of stiff, green lily points
fingering the clear *azul celeste* overhead.
She thinks how day after dry day, the plants cry
their tequila sugars, as he sloshes his sour words,
and she spills her salted tears. He hears how
the *machetes* of his lies have severed their dreams
like a *quiote*, before blessings could blossom.
She remembers when he sipped her urgent kisses
like *aguamiel*, instead of bitterly spitting
the seeds of his lists, his longings, his leavings.
He admits he will always need her to make her smile.
Turning to face one another in a splash of sun on stone,
they form a makeshift altar: four feet on the hardscrabble ground.
Softening to a bride, she offers her blue heart as *agave sazon.*
Ripened and ready, it is his, she says, theirs, a sacred gift
to be crushed, heated, distilled into the syrup of tender mercies.
Humbled to a devoted *jardinero*, he vows a better harvest, a next
season, a good year. Walking the rocky road
back to the village, two saints with doubts thick as honey,
they hold on to hope and each other, drink deeply
a new, clear spirit that, like Jalisco's tequila, is *auténtico*;
like Oaxaca's mezcal, *con gusano.*

Margarita

Jerry Bradley

Margaritas are my drink for luck,
their briny brims the taste
of sweat after love and stems
like the legs of starlets
frozen in the moment
before they open in all my dreams.

In Mexico when we drank our healths
I kept us all well, the ones
who'd tossed their hearts like dice
and stood eyeball with the snake
or been ridden like boxcars to the grave.
We cursed our scars but kept pistols
in the car to be safe.

Absurd and possessed, we drank through
heedless youth and lived. Now
we drink for luck—good,
bad, and indifferent—
and to waken to find you here
is to taste again the curious heart
of cactus on my tongue.

Nathan Brown, "Cowboy Buddha" from Doc Martin's in Taos

Your Margaritas
David Rains

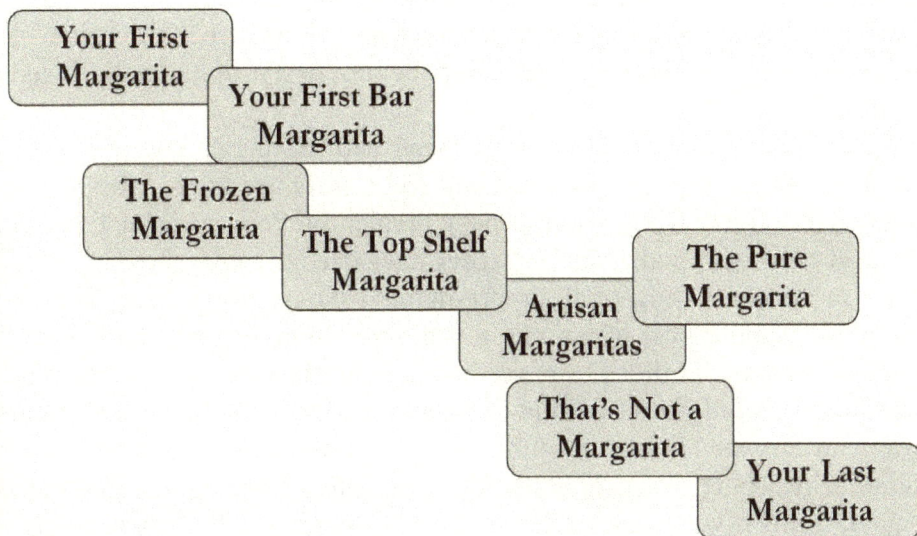

Your First Margarita

Your First Margarita is probably an unguided excursion into the world of alcohol, taken during your youth. You may well consume it at a party, from a plastic cup. It will likely be a cheap version, as available funds need to go a long way if everyone is going to feel good. Your First Margarita(s) may also be associated with your first hangover, or with a group of friends, or just a general feeling of fun, and it has therefore become the drink of acceptance or avoidance (if it happened to make you sick) for many people from their first tart-but-sweet-with-a-kick sip.

Your First Margarita at a Bar

This is your first professionally mixed Margarita, not that that's necessarily saying much. (It could also be Your First Margarita as described above.) You probably come to order this drink with little knowledge of all the potential variation, perversion of the style per se, and price ranges possible, depending on your location. If there are no choices to be made, then so be it—you are likely in for some sour mix with well tequila, and even (horrors!) a splash of Sprite, served in a salt-rimmed glass or even a plastic cup. These kinds of bars offer their own charm. (It is possible, though quite unlikely, that your first Margarita is at a really good bar that takes the approach that there is only one way they intend to serve the drink, and so your lack of choice means you are in the hands of a dictatorial purist. But that's unlikely to be your first professionally mixed Margarita.)

Otherwise, you are likely to be faced with decisions you are quite unprepared for, and perhaps you will feel a little pressure. After all, to engage in inquiry when a bar is busy breaks the flow. In what I would suspect to be the majority of bars, they have tried to make choosing easy for you with a listing of their pre-defined concoctions. They all say something about you of course, a topic for another essay altogether, perhaps like one of those tests you see in magazines at the supermarket checkout that tell you what kind of lover/friend/wingman you are by the way you answer about ten multiple choice questions. Choosing "Top-Shelf," Strawberry Frozen, or the El Diablo all define you in some way. Again, if this is your first time you won't really know what you're doing, and isn't that how we all learn best?

The Frozen Margarita

We'll never know the origins of this drink, but blenders and ice have been together for many years now. (However, the frozen Margarita machine was invented by Dallas restaurateur Mariano Martinez, and indeed his first machine, now at the Hacienda Ranch on Dallas' Skillman Avenue, once sat in the Smithsonian, a fact which adds considerable gravitas to this account.) Perhaps the origins lie with some sleepy drinkers the morning after looking for a little hair of the dog and finding the frozen remains of their previous night's beverage on the porch stoop.

We all know the frozen Margarita comes in flavors, strawberry being the dominant alternative choice. If the machines are set up for swirl, then there's that yin and yang looking option, or the "dot," a dollop of the contrasting choice on top.

Regardless, the Frozen Margarita is a widely accepted choice, one that usually implies a higher fun quotient whenever served (at a bar, or imagine what a rented frozen Margarita machine engenders), and is almost never about premium ingredients. It's about refreshment. These are best discovered on hot days. And a curious development in the last few decades is the "floater," a splash of tequila applied to the surface of your frozen drink, to be consumed as an initial shot, or stirred in to fortify the experience. Why not?

The Top-Shelf Margarita

This is a hackneyed term by now, but it persists. Formerly, "Top-Shelf" meant an upgrade to premium ingredients, which were the best in the house, and often literally sitting on the top shelf. Usually, one of the three or four (at best) premium tequilas, possibly real lime juice, and Gran Marnier did the trick, served on the rocks. But this was before the Tequila Revolution. There are now tequilas that stand proudly among the single malt scotches and small-batch whiskeys, and are priced just as dearly, and these are unlikely to find themselves in a mixed drink, so the bartender may not need to reach very high to make your "Top Shelf" drink.

Once, ordering a Top Shelf meant you were a high roller, someone who wanted the best and didn't mind paying for it. Nowadays, it could just as easily mean you're a bargain hunter, as the Top Shelf may well be the establishment's mid-tier offering.

The Artisan Margarita

These are being made in bars, restaurants, and homes all over the globe, and are usually accompanied by a sometimes well-deserved sense of pride tending to snobbery. This would be the time to launch into an essay on agave syrup, and I advise someone to make this a dissertation topic, but suffice it to say that even the sweeteners in these drinks are potentially esoteric. Reposado tequilas, fresh exotic citrus, and even flavored salts may appear.

The Pure Margarita

Plato believed in forms as the highest reality, and so the Platonic Margarita might simply be the blending of tequila, triple sec, and fresh lime or lemon juice over ice, but there must be something more (or less) to make this the ideal. You might be surprised to find the Margarita is not the most popular tequila cocktail in its purported country of origin, Mexico. The Paloma is. And of course, the origin of the Margarita is lost among multiple contending claims to its invention. So whatever the first Margarita was, an ideal has emerged that gives form in the corporeal world to endless variation. You may well fancy yourself a Margarita "purist," and if so, you know the real thing when you drink it, and can perhaps smile at the recognition in a way that most cannot.

That's Not a Margarita

There are some variations that just go too far to carry the name. While there are no hard-and-fast boundaries, one might pause in the presence of a "Mayogarita," a Japanese version including mayonnaise, or the presence of cucumber, avocado, exotic liqueurs, chocolate, etc. and ask oneself what you're doing. Surely such a concoction (abomination?) calling itself by the name of the simple but beautiful Mexican girl that may have inspired all the madness would be a drink neither the inventor or the inspiration would recognize.

Your Last Margarita

Someday, you will have Your Last Margarita. You may, of course, never know while you're drinking that this one drink in your hand is it. Or you might: you could successfully swear off drinking, or the cocktail itself, or perhaps know that you no longer can have one. But probably you won't know. So it makes sense to enjoy your next one, and each one that follows as if it's your last.

order

Milton Brasher-Cunningham

I have
enough
in my life
already
on the rocks—

make mine
frozen
with salt.

How to Make a Long Island Iced Tea
Millard Dunn

Very **G**ood **T**ime
To **R**emember **S**weethearts
(**C**autiously).

In equal parts:
Vodka, **G**in, **T**equila,
Triple Sec, **R**um, **S**weet and Sour
(**C**oca-Cola for color
or taste, if you like.)

Dias de Las Margaritas
Karla K. Morton

For years, we gathered from across
the states—our yearly pilgrimage,
craving salsa and salted margaritas;
the cool, worn edges of limestone,

lifting strollers up river archways,
and back down the other side;
market confetti-eggs caught
in tow-headed hair.

Come fall, our oldest will scatter
like spooked quail—
into a world as wide as the wind;
years of enchiladas pumping their muscles;

stories we've told and re-told
burned into their brains—
music to spin in their heads years later,
before sleep; harmonies of aunts and uncles

and late-night laughter...
songs whisked through Alamo walls
laid open in the dark,
like jawbones, ancient and pale.

Christine Russell

Before Goodbye
David Meischen

River air swirls thick with voices.
Salt crystals crumble against my lips,
sugared limes, tequila's amber warmth
drifting us into something like ease, jostled
by syllables slipped loose from syntax
light as fingertips fluttering the tablecloth.
Tonight everything is possible, even love,
compelling as the apparition of promise, rippling,
wavering in the nightlights on the water,
flecks of color shimmying the night air,
your touch light as memory. A whisper. Listen.

Tequila's Accomplice
Kellie Salome

A lime can look innocent.

Tequila never does.

A pair of limes presents a question: Components? Tequila has an answer.

A group of limes suggests a plan. Tequila always has a plan.

So start with the tequila. We talk about good tequila with the language of fine wine, commenting on *bouquet* and *earth* and *minerals*—words that lend themselves to an organic poetry. There is a reason. Pick well. I prefer *Don Eduardo Reposado*, which has nice spice and a vibrant finish. But this is an act of individual expression, something you can do selfishly and without guilt; your favorite tequila for your best margarita.

Take a moment and smell the tequila, unlocked from its pretty prison. Does it make you wince and cause your eyes to water? Does it smell like butter, or flowers, or hay? Or does it carry some essence of all these at once? Does it seem suspiciously innocuous?

Tequila can make you feel worthy of love. Show appreciation. Don't skimp. Be generous with the pour: a healthy ounce and a half. Layer a half ounce of clear Cointreau over that. Some people prefer Grand Marnier, but I find the heavier orange invasive. Again, your preference should dominate your choice. Add a splash of simple syrup (equal parts sugar and water, boil to dissolve). If you forego the simple syrup, use an extra half ounce of Cointreau. A good margarita is a balancing act; tip too far into one direction, disaster ensues.

Next, the innocent limes. The number varies, depending on the size and quantity of juice extruded. Two ripe, medium-sized limes per drink is a good average, freshly squeezed with a metal press so the oil oozes from the skin. That slight bitterness will serve you well. A subtle perfume, if you will. The lingering scent of something pure, unspoiled: the adolescent lime before the sudden marriage to mature tequila.

There are rules.

No blenders—ever. If you want it frozen, you might as well go ahead and buy the pre-mix and a bottle of shitty tequila and start your hangover. Just know that you were told. Just understand that you did this to yourself.

Use a shaker tin: to mix directly in the glass is to ruin the mysterious chemistry achieved only with that rough motion that breaks particles from the ice and best resolves the bite of tequila in a frigid environment, that lovingly expresses the deep bruise of lime with a gratitude that cannot be achieved with a mere stir. The shaker tin consummates the marriage in a violent bed: brutal tequila, battered lime, shattered ice. Some things must be broken open to blend.

Only the salt should remain separate, coarse and stinging. The salt should be a fine crust, not a heavy embankment on the lip of the glass. The glass itself plays an important role: not one of those spindly-stemmed, shallow bowls, but one with a flat bottom that stays put when you set it down; one that is thick enough so that the heat of your hand doesn't warm the ice through it. Ten ounces is sufficient.

The ice is important as well: hefty cubes that chip when shaken but don't dissolve too quickly. You want them floating, embraced by liquid, not liquid themselves. Not yet.

Ice does chuckle, by the way; particularly in the company of good tequila.

So: good tequila, Cointreau, blood of the limes, simple syrup, and stout ice, all in the tin.

Next: shake, hard. Be unambiguous about the damage you inflict. Embrace the violence of the act, but briefly. Prolonged abuse is unnecessary. A deliberate count to ten should do it, like keeping your eyes closed while everyone changes position in a game of Red Light. Transfer to the waiting glass.

A note: some people like to pour over fresh ice, but I believe that hard work and sacrifice should be rewarded and that the chipped ice has earned a place. If you agree, keep a strainer handy. Pour away from the glass's edge to avoid washing the salt away. Slowly shift what ice you need down into the pool. Try not to splash. Are these instructions too precise? Ah, but some things must be executed precisely: the stroke of a brush, a sustained note, a pirouette. Art requires attention. Let the mixture rise like flood waters until it hovers just below the line of salt. Decoration with an unmolested lime wedge is optional, but not necessary.

Take a moment to appreciate what you have done.

Now, sample your effort: touch your tongue to the salted rim, feel the contraction in the rush of saliva. There is more to tighten your mouth around. The comparison to fine wine continues. Take a sip and let the concoction roll around to bathe your tongue, wash your cheeks, and coat your teeth. The roof of your mouth will twitch away from the cold sting of lime, of salt, of delicate poison. Breathe in; let yourself breathe through the drinking. This path involves surrender. The smell of softened limes, wet and reduced, should be in your nose. Salt should briefly drift on the flat of your tongue with each sip.

Reminiscence comes with tequila. Though heartbreak is inevitable, tequila recalls that early flushed romance, when every moment before the first touch is unbearable and every moment after only the burning before the ashes. Tequila makes a bonfire of memories. You will find your mind turning inward, following the path of a good margarita as it warms you: your throat, your chest, your heart. Note: a bad margarita makes you cringe; why would you want to follow that? Follow warmth and memory. Initially what you will recall is every loving moment, relived with a cold throat and a warm belly; later all you will discover is what you have lost. But that is later, a few indulgences down. First there is this: tart sting of lime and salt, sweet breath of sugar and citrus. This is how tequila conquers—in the company of others. The components of a good margarita become tequila's accomplice. And tequila always has a plan. You can fight with it, love it desperately, weep over it, celebrate it, and knock your head open on the floor from it. Do not make the mistake of discounting such affection as temporary. Do not view it as shallow, or unreturned, for that matter. Tequila is a patiently devious friend, one who rests safely on the ground and taunts you, standing on the hive dive, to jump. You jump; of course you do. You seek escape, without always knowing from what or to where, without comprehension that you run faster in the direction of your doom, your pain, your worst flinching moments with each sip. You leap and fall. But after the leap the long fall is exhilarating: You are briefly in flight—closer than you imagined possible—and when the deep pool of oblivion closes over your head you smile and sink, forgetting the need for air for a time.

Their Fourth Ph.D. Discuss Party
James Ragan

Margaritas drip heavy off their lips,
a strain on the loss of spoons
in conversation, a quiver at the knees
where the committee sits, itching

China, a point to be made
on Pound—these aging scholars
in the exam room, proving oral delivery
the test of stamina

for the mind, for the etymology
of sounds on the upper lip,
a concentration surviving thoughts of meat
balls and shrimp. They are limp

in body, at the knees, their plates
a pound of lead. They have prayed ahead
for strength to pass this test,
this long toss of the word "Moloch!"

across each skull, each ball
a brain to pick, each itch a foreign tongue
to the men who rule contra-diction,
"short of the mark, the next time they'll drink
tequila."

José Cuervo

Cindy Jordan (Country Music Song of the Year 1983)

Well it's Sunday Mornin' and the sun is shinin'
In my eye that is open and my head is spinnin'
Was the life of the party I can't stop grinnin'
I had to much Tequila last night

José Cuervo you are a friend of mine
I like to drink you with a little salt and lime
Did I kiss all the cowboys?
Did I shoot out the lights?
Did I dance on the bar?
Did I start any fights?

Now wait a minute things don't look to familiar
Who is this cowboy who's sleepin' beside me?
He's awfully cute, but how'd I get his shirt on?
I had to much Tequila last night

José Cuervo you are a friend of mine
I like to drink you with a little salt and lime
Did I kiss all the cowboys?
Did I shoot out the lights?
Did I dance on the bar?
Did I start any fights?

All those little shooters how I love to drink 'em down
Come on bartender let's have another round
Well the music is playing and my spirits are high
Tomorrow might be painful but tonight we're gonna fly

José Cuervo you are a friend of mine
I like to drink you with a little salt and lime
Every time we get together I sure have a good time
You're my friend You're the best
Mi amigo Cuervo
José Cuervo you are a friend of mine

I like to drink you with a little salt and lime
Did I kiss all the cowboys?
Did I shoot out the lights?
Did I dance on the bar?
Did I start any fights?

Grace

Beth Robinson

Tequila was always my favorite
    Or was it vodka?
No frozen drinks, please
    nothing with too many ingredients.
    Just a margarita on the rocks
       not much ice
       and some days
           no salt.

I recall some fascination with the poor drowned worm
    by high school boys.
Do invertebrates experience intoxication?
    Or would that presume brain cells to start with?

But the sideways smile of one
    beautiful dark-skinned man with a bottle in his hand and
    who-knows-what in his heart...

Thank You, God.

There's a reason I haven't tasted tequila in more than twenty-two years.

Good Tequila, Naked Women, and Blue Bell Ice Cream
Terry Dalrymple

Good tequila is like a good woman. That's what Rusty Cargile told me on many occasions. Good tequila, he'd say, is like a good woman. Treat her right and she'll treat you right, but abuse her and she'll make you suffer.

At sixteen I ignored his advice about the tequila and suffered in more ways than one. I didn't make that mistake again. But at twenty-eight I guess I forgot the part about the good woman, and I said some things I should never have said.

Sally Gaines left my apartment crying and didn't come back, and after three days I was suffering way more than I did from that tequila. She didn't answer calls and didn't return them. That third night I thought about killing myself. Then I thought about getting shit-faced drunk. And then I thought about going to Rusty Cargile's ranch a hundred and seventy miles southwest of Dallas, where I lived at the time.

I grew up only about twenty miles from Rusty's place. When I was fourteen, my dad died of a heart attack. Two years later, my mom remarried. The guy was okay and I didn't resent the marriage, but I didn't want to spend any more time than I had to in the house where they were husband and wife. So I went looking for an after-school job. A friend of my dad's told me about Rusty, said he ranched alone and might use help with jobs around the place. He worked me like a mule, but he also taught me how to do a lot of things I didn't even know I could do. He was a gruff old bastard, but he never treated me bad. And he was a hell of a lot smarter than he let on most times. So when I graduated I stayed on with him for two years, figuring if he was that smart without a college degree I could be too. What I did later get smart about is how much more I could make working construction in Dallas. But I stayed in touch with Rusty and visited him once or twice a year.

I arrived at his ranch house late in the evening, maybe eleven, and found him on his porch literally howling at the moon.

"Rusty Cargile," I called out, "you are a troubled soul."

"Hah," he hollered back. "No trouble I know that can't be cured by Doctor Don Eduardo."

"I could use a little doctoring myself," I said, "if you're of a mind to share."

"Donny Farmer, what the hell you doing at my house?"

"Just saying hi."

"Uh-huh," he said in that way I knew so well. He drew the syllables out to emphasize the irony in his response. Had he said words, they would have been something like, "That's a damn lie, but I won't pry."

"Don't suppose you've got an extra room for a couple of days?" I asked. The hollow wooden sound my boots made on his porch steps seemed somehow comforting.

"Shit, boy, I got a houseful of rooms for a lifetime. Come on in, bring your girlfriend, raise a family."

"Just me," I said. Up on the creaky wooden porch, I accepted the glass he offered, took a sip, then another before handing it back. I smacked my lips and whistled. "Mighty fine tequila."

"Don Eduardo Añejo, my boy."

"You're howling at the moon," I said. "You been abusing the don?"

"Hell no. You ever known me to?"

In truth, I never had. Good tequila. Don't shoot it, he'd say. Don't swig it. And for God's sake don't mix it with shit. Sip it, always sip it.

"Go on," he said. He nodded toward the screen door. "Get yourself a glass."

He kept his liquor in an old cedar cabinet he'd made himself many years before. The glasses would be there, I knew. Paper cups and plastic cups in the kitchen. You could drink tea or water from them. But never tequila. Good tequila needed good glasses. I fetched one and returned to the rocking chair next to his, something else he had made long before I knew him. He made the rockers when he and his wife bought and moved to the ranch. They were made for rocking babies to sleep on cool spring evenings just like this one, watching the stars come out, listening to the night sounds.

One of those babies had died at three, and Rusty's wife had taken the other away when she left. So far as I knew, Rusty had never heard from either one of them again,

Rusty poured into my glass and raised his. We toasted silently and each sipped. "You never told me, Rusty. What happened to your wife?"
He sipped again and stared out at the dark shadows of oaks beyond the porch. "You know what I like?" he asked.

"You like sippin' good tequila," I said.

"Damn right I do." He sipped again. "Good tequila is like a good woman."

"So you told me."

40

"So where is that good woman of yours?"

"Not sure," I said. "Separate vacations, you know?"

"Uh-huh."

Damn him, I thought, and his insight. "So what about your wife?" I reached into my shirt pocket for cigarettes. I had quit smoking two years before at Sally's urging but had bought a pack when I gassed up on the way to Rusty's. I peeled off the cellophane, flipped the box open, and pulled out the foil flap. I stuffed the cellophane and foil into my pocket. Rusty hated trash lying around. I pulled a cigarette out of the box with my teeth, then realized I had no lighter. "Got a light?" I asked.

As a rule he didn't smoke either, but sometimes, on the porch sipping tequila, he'd puff a cigar or smoke a cigarette or two. He pulled some paper matches from his shirt pocket. Before handing them to me he said, "Got a cigarette?"

I handed him the pack and he handed me the matches. After lighting up, I passed the matches back. "So," I said, "what about your wife?"

His match flared and he sucked the flame into the end of his cigarette. He shook the match out and set it on the small wooden table between us. "So," he said, then paused to inhale deeply. He blew the smoke out into the darkness. "What about your job?"

"It'll be there," I said.

"Uh-huh."

He was right. Miss a day or two in construction and you'll find someone in your place when you return. I had missed two days without even calling in.

"What about you?" I asked. "How's ranching?"

"A walk through hell, son. A goddamn walk through hell."

"Can't be that bad."

"Shit. Brower brought his boys over and bailed my hay. Charged twice what he did last year."

"Times are tough. He's got to make a living."

"Shit." He emptied his glass and reached for the bottle. "You know what I like?" he said.

To keep up I drained my glass and tilted it toward him for a pour. "You like sippin' good tequila."

"Yeah," he said, "but something else. I like girlie magazines."

"Jesus, Rusty, don't tell me any more."

"No, shit, I don't mean anything nasty. But those girls are so young and firm and soft and buxom and beautiful. Makes you believe in Jesus."

"I don't think he's the publisher."

He leaned forward to peer out from under the roof and howl at the moon. The rocking chair tipped a little too far and he tumbled off the porch. He hit the ground and the breath whooshed out of him. I didn't budge. If there was anything he hated it was people thinking he needed help. I sipped from the replenished glass of tequila. "You alive?"

"Yeah," he wheezed, still gasping for breath.

"Anything broken?"

"Not so I can tell." His hands appeared first on the edge of the porch. He pulled up onto his knees. "Maybe my pride a little."

"Rusty Cargile, you are definitely a troubled soul."

"Shit, boy," he said and then grunted from the effort of standing up. "We're all troubled souls. Me, you, that pretty girlfriend of yours, those lovely naked girls that make me believe in Jesus. Hell, everybody in the whole goddamn world is a troubled soul." He grunted again when he hiked a leg onto the porch and pulled himself up by a post. "Life is hard sometimes, Donny. But you know what? Pretty much it's okay."

His cigarette had been crushed out in the fall. He stepped into the house. "I don't know," I said, more to the night than to him. "Nothing much seems pretty okay to me." He came back with an empty green bean can, into which he dropped the butt. He dropped the spent match in there, too, settled into his rocker, and set the can on the little table. I took a last drag and crushed my smoke out in the can.

He looked at me hard for a few seconds, then picked up the cigarette box and flipped the top open. He pulled out a cigarette. "She left," he said, "because I told her to." He looked at the cigarette, rolled it back and forth between thumb and forefinger. "I've done a lot of dumb things in my life, but that's the goddamn dumbest."

"Why'd you do it?"

"Hell, I don't know. She pissed me off, I guess." He finally struck a match and lit the cigarette. "Why'd you?" he said.

"Why'd I what?"

"Do whatever it is you did wrong."

I reached for the bottle and poured a couple fingers. "*She* was wrong," I said, but I neither sounded nor felt convinced. I tilted the bottle toward him and poured when he raised his glass.

"I'd bet my ass," he said, "that you were wronger."

We sipped and just sat listening to the night. A deep-voiced owl whooed from somewhere in the oaks. A whippoorwill called out as if responding. "You ever hear from her," I asked. "Or your boy?"

His cigarette glowed bright when he dragged on it. "I hear from those whippoorwills every night. I like them." He took another drag. "Hey, you know what else I like?"

"No, but I believe you're going to tell me."

"Ice cream. Vanilla. That good kind, you know, Blue Bell."

"Ice cream, huh?"

"Yeah. It's so rich and creamy and you roll it over your tongue and then let it slide down your throat all soft and cool." He stubbed out the cigarette, took a sip of tequila.

"You're a strange man, Rusty Cargile." I stood up and stretched, then walked to the other end of the porch. I leaned against a post and looked off into the distance where Rusty's largest tank reflected light from the quarter moon. That light was enough to make clear the outlines of mesquites scattered around the pond. Scrubs mostly, and few larger ones. The bank, I knew, was dull brown, pocked with hoof prints and littered with cow shit. But in the middle of the night with that moonlight glinting on the water and forming outlines of the trees, it looked like an oasis.

"How long you staying, Donny?" Rusty asked from behind me.

"You got any work?" I said without turning around.

"Hell yes. For you and twenty more like you."

"Just me," I said.

"Then I got work that'll last you to your grave. If it don't put you there first."

I turned around and stepped back across the porch, but near the steps I paused. I stared at the dark shape of my truck. "You know," I said, "I should get my phone, probably try to call Sally." My boots going down the steps made that same comforting hollow clunk.

"You know what I like?" Rusty said.

I turned back toward him. "I guess I'm about to hear," I said.

"Church bells."

"Never figured you for a church man, Rusty."

"I'm not. But I like those bells." I heard the neck of the Don Eduardo clink against the rim of his glass. "Some Sunday mornings I'll drive to that little church on the outskirts of town. Catholic, I think. Or maybe Episcopalian."

"Yeah," I said. "I know the one."

"I'll roll down the windows and just sit waiting for those bells. That first clang of the clapper sort of jars you, you know? But then the sound softens and hangs all clear and ethereal in the air."

I laughed. "Ethereal!"

"That's right, ethereal. It means—"

"I know what it means. I just never heard you use such a word."

"There's a hell of a lot more than that you've never heard."

I stepped back onto the porch to get a cigarette from the pack, lit it, then returned to the steps and sat on the top one. "I never heard an ethereal church bell that lasted very long," I said.

"And I never heard one," he said, "that could be unrung. They can be re-rung, but never exactly the same. You know, given wind variables and all."

"Wind variables, huh?"

"Just the same," he said, "it's kind of nice to remember."

I sat and smoked and stared out at the shape of my truck. Inside it were the one small bag I had packed, a bottle of Patron Reposado I'd brought as a gift for Rusty, and my cell phone. We didn't talk until my cigarette was a nub and I said, "You know what I like? I like sipping your good tequila."

He chuckled. "Well, then, sit your ass up here and sip some."

I stood up and looked at the moon. I leaned my head back and howled. Then I returned to the rocking chair and stubbed out my cigarette. He poured and handed me my glass. I sipped. "You know what else I like?" I asked.

"Nope," he said. "But I expect I'm going to find out."

Laurence Musgrove

TEX

TEX MEX

TEX FLEX

TEX NECKS

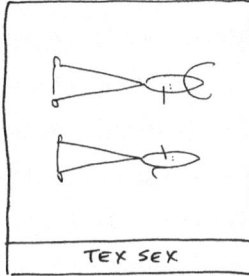

TEX SEX

TEX TEXTS

TEX WRECKS

TEX EXCESS

TEX EX

TEX

Musgrove

45

Tequila Talk
James Hoggard

He drank tequila neat
and never had bad stomach aches
those years in San Miguel
when all his paintings had
an empty space, a hole, some said,
a nod toward emptiness.
Was something missing in his soul,
but who, I thought, could know? —
and kept that thought until
one night he gave a gallery talk,
and one event, he said,
made all his life and work make sense:
that time, he said, *when Dad*
and I stood back to back
within the cyclone of a fight,
a bar fight, too, our quick
fists cocked then swinging hard,
and I knew then we never know
what love is like until
you find your joy as you go back
to back with your own dad,
go wild within a big bar fight.

Blue Margaritas
Carol Hamilton

Chimayo restaurant, magic mud nearby
and our table long, the pitchers frosty,
our thirst whetted by the red dust
that coated us riding in a pickup bed.
Hard days digging, crouched,
tiny paintbrushes dusting away
at silt that cradled Navajo artifacts.
My drink tasted so good! No idea
of the blue liqueur to fortify
the tequila. It hit so hard!
No idea how strong....
no idea how big the pitcher...
or when I'd ever
feel so good again!
Heavenly color,
that salt-rimed blue.

Tequila Dragons

Steven Schroeder, Yang Qian, and Mary Ann O'Donnell

Tequila
龙舌的花
开在兰色龙舌上
的 Tequila
冷血的兰色
喷出冰晶一样灸的火
Tequila
兰龙舌喝下龙舌沉沉睡去
在上一年的地壳下
整流出火山
沙漠已经从海中浮现

在沙丘深处还有几支活着的龙舌花
藏着地下的甘泉
留给那些跋涉万里的旅人
走到迷途的终点

tequila
long she de hua blooms
on dragon's orchid tongue
tequila
cold blooded agave
spits sparks of fire
tequila
dragon's orchid tongue drinks
long she de hua into deep deep sleep
down in earth's ancient crust
fermenting volcanoes
and desert sands floating
on the face of the ocean

in this floating desert
dragon tongued agave live
hiding sweet springs deep underground
for those on a ten thousand mile journey
trudging to confusion's end

2

orchid dragon tongue spirit

burns the way a snake bite burns
turns the way a falcon turns

thrives the way an orchid does
on wind, rising. rising, it is

all we are, dust
on wind. blue agave
flowers yellow, draws

ideas like bats: we
see in them both mice

and birds, a dozen
years of hearts,

sweet fires that rise
as a volcano does,

petals we pluck to pose
questions about love.

desert dry, we drink
to lose our minds

and hope a poem
will find us.

3

a toast for old times

raise a cup of kindness
raise a cup of what is

distilled from purple dragon tongues
rooted in the fire in the belly of the earth

follow every round
with something
salty, something

tart. bring the spirit on
and never tip your golden cup
empty to the moon

Mary Ann O'Donnell

Write about Tequila
Hannah Rappaport

Write about tequila. The final note on my to do list today after deposit checks, buy bath mat, and deliver the book on Paracelsus to a friend who is forging her learning toward alchemy, the science and art of transformation—materially from base metal to gold, spiritually from discord, clinging, and suffering to full-hearted soulfulness.

Write about tequila. It will have to be a stream of consciousness because I've never thought a whole lot about tequila, other than to order a margarita with one poet friend or another.

Pour some tequila. I found some El Jimador in the liquor cabinet. No selection of tequila to write home about. I'm staying in the home of some friends, taking care of their two cats. They seem to be rum people. There is no Scotch.

Take a sip of tequila, ah warm from tongue to chest, and my heart expands with the images and feelings of this blessed evening where nothing much has happened. I took a brisk walk in the first frosty days of winter-on-her-way—snow atop Taos Mountain. A picture is worth a thousand words. Thanks to the photographer for capturing that beauty. He couldn't go wrong with that majesty. None of us—we can't go wrong. Life is blessed including our suffering. The slant of sundown brilliant dazzling, the image of heavy gray clouds menacingly leaning against peaks, closing in on colors—golds, reds, grays—and below, the peaks still green, punctuated by golden Quaking Aspen, leaves clutching to their last life through a week of frosty nights and wild winds. Not afraid to die, just loving what is left, the goldenness of their being. They will return. Life is eternal. Only delusion craps out—can't maintain itself inside the splendor of reality.

I'll forget this image, dissolved into the matrix of beauty that is Taos, glad someone caught it on film; though his picture will never divulge the full experience of cold legs inside thin pants thinking of how warm it might feel when I sit down to take a sip and write about tequila.

In the house, warmed by radiant heat rising from the floor, the cat drifts, eyes closed, leg outstretched from the back of the sofa. The red has gone now from the sky. The wind chimes play an evening raga. I live now in a golden moment, no burning red, no ashen black of the alchemical athanor, the caldron where spirit person is forged. The work I've done with heart, mind, and body have forged a soul that needs no drunkenness to escape from pain. A warm sip of tequila is just nice on a cold evening and I think yes, the poets who have praised liquor de agave are right about tequila.

McAllen, Room 263

Juan Manuel Perez

Mescal on my breath
Ideas on my mind
I didn't say they were good
I didn't say they were good
Sitting naked on the fancy couch
Pissed off at myself
Sometime during the night
God gave me a great poem
I was too drunk to write it down
I surely pissed it out of my brain
Now it's gone forever
It was beauty, profound
Trying my damnest to recall it
It's eight o'clock in the morning
This is all I can do
This is all I can do
Ideas on my mind
I didn't say they were good
No, I didn't say they were good

Sonoran Monsoon Season
July 4, 2010
Audell Shelburne

> *I don't know why bad ideas*
> *spread faster than good ones,*
> *but they do.*
> —David Sedaris

Folks sip margaritas and beer,
smoke babyback ribs, gorge themselves
on sweet corn and watermelon,
clamoring for the yearly fireworks show,
patriotic bombs bursting in air
to celebrate the unalienable rights
to send aliens back where they came from
and to treat everyone as an illegal
just for breathing the air of liberty
in the land of the free and home of the brave.
Storm clouds build on the mountains,
gusts whipping through the valley
shaking ancient saguaro to the roots.

Audell Shelburne

Tequila Chicken
Barrie Scardino

This recipe takes three days to make.

Day 1 – Invite about 6 of your craziest friends over for dinner three nights hence. If you don't have any friends, street people love this recipe (or any other). Go to the liquor store and buy about 10 different tequilas, then taste test to decide which one to use.

Day 2 – Take two Advil for your hangover and go to the grocery store. Come home, take two more Advil, and make the marinade. (see below)

Day 3 – Clean up your house, set the table, and put out the left-over tequilas from Day 1 with shot glasses. This recipe is fantastic if everyone is drunk before they eat it. Cook.

6 chicken breasts (or one for each person)—if you are cheap, you can use
    4 pounds of wings
1 cup, at least, of your chosen tequila
½ cup frozen orange juice concentrate
Zest of 1 large lime (if you don't have a fancy zester, just grate the whole
    rind)
Juice of 2 limes (for more juice, put limes in microwave for 20 sec. before
    cutting them)
4 cloves minced garlic
1 ½ tsp freshly ground black pepper (coarse is good)
1 ½ tsp salt (Kosher or sea salt)
4 tbsp minced cilantro (don't use dried cilantro, it tastes like grass)

Combine orange juice concentrate, tequila, lemon zest, lime juice, black pepper, garlic, cilantro, and salt in a great vat. *Do not drink!* Put this marinade and the chicken into a large container or plastic bag and seal. Refrigerate overnight.

Drain the chicken; discard the marinade. If you live in West Texas, grill the chicken over a mesquite fire. If not, you will have to rely on charcoal or gas. To keep the meat moist, spray lightly several times with a good cooking oil, such as PAM olive oil. Turn frequently and cook until tender (time depends on kind and size of the chicken—should be about 25 minutes, give or take).

If you have any tequila left, serve the dinner with margaritas; Mexican beer works too.

For side dishes try red rice (find a recipe on the internet) and your favorite salad (we like one with pears, pine nuts, blue cheese, and vinaigrette). If you are feeling creative you could invent a tequila salad dressing and submit it to the publisher for the second edition of this book.

For dessert we highly recommend the Tasty Tequila Teacakes found in this very volume! And to accompany them, go ahead and break out your good tequila (that we know you have hidden away from your guests) for a few parting shots!

ENJOY!

Two Dogs Howling at the Moon

For Rusty Wier 1944-2009

David Parsons

I will always remember the last time I saw you,
at your *angel's*, Tricia's crowded Plano townhouse

and how, after our four hours of harmoniously
catching-up on thirty some odd years of lost time,

I read you my poem *The Pride*, about that pack
we ran with—we thought we were lions, we were

more wolves or stray dogs—reliving those old stories
of growing up together wild in the enigmatic sixties

in South Austin, like our Tequila drinking contest
when I came home from the Marines, how I passed

out hearing you strumming to *Rave On*, learning
later, you had quickly followed me to the darkness

falling dead-drunk onto your beat up old guitar,
like some faithful warrior falling on his sword.

As our visiting ebbed, you played for me the second
of your three new songs, saying, *I'm still writing—*

*can't stop doing that one thing—we're like those two
old dogs in my song, David, we writers just keep barking*

and howling at that ole' moon, your voice still
inimitably valved despite the chemo and the thousands

of songs poured out like manna to the many hungering
audiences of the nightlife you so loved and I remember

at that moment thinking how Li Po is said to have so

adored that great luminous orb that he perished, when

after a night of heavy drinking, he fell into the lake
attempting to embrace the dazzling antediluvian body, tumbling

head-long and alone into the deep ink of oblivion,
or perhaps, the masked reflections of an eternal light

and how you, after sailing through countless gigs
and seas of Agave, one complimentary shot at a time,

were now arduously floundering to make the best of each
of these last painfully clumsy egregious moments,

like you always have, with that distinctive dancing
twinkle in the weathered squint of those smiling blue

eyes, eyes still fully alive in my memory, still dancing—

I suppose every human passion holds within its core
the germ of something lethal to its being and yet,

somehow, interwoven with the potential of rapture.
Tonight the sheer linen curtains of my bedroom seem

to be tossed by the blurring energy of the moonlight
bouncing glowing stones across the dark water of our pool

as the ceiling fan circles in its perpetual waving orbits
and I can hear my daughter's tiny lap dog underneath

my small dinghy of a bed gnawing like memories
on a T-bone scrap from dinner, he is at that phase

where all the meat is flayed away and one can only
hear the sound of bone against bone as he is working

into a rhythm in his ceaseless mastication, creating
his own unique kind of wild, raw and satisfying music.

Five Acres North of the Red River
Jim Spurr

It is summer.
She is dancing
slowly and alone.
Barefoot in her unfenced
backyard.
Listening to quiet
country music.
Eyes closed, knees together
and holding her arms high.
She clings to a long, slim,
cigarette
as she chases margaritas
with Miller High Life
trying to stay
a little intoxicated.
Just enough
to love the wait
for George Strait
to come riding into her
tanned, bare,
...summer arms.

Lips Like Pink Elephants
Andrew Geyer

The bar on the patio at Pat O'Brien's in San Antonio was topped with oak, stained dark. The patio was long and narrow, and three of the walls were wood-paneled, stained dark like the bar; but the afternoon sun poured through the plate glass windows that filled the wall between the bar and the courtyard. Out among the courtyard tables, a fountain splashed and played in the afternoon sun. Plate glass doors guarded the entrance to the courtyard, keeping the cool air in the patio bar and the flies outside. The American Literature professor sat on a barstool nursing his second happy hour pint of Guinness. Next to him a bleach-blonde in a hot pink dress, which perfectly matched the hot pink lipstick on her engorged lips, sucked the last of the hurricane the professor had bought her through double straws. Then she looked away, out into the courtyard.

"Another hurricane?" the professor asked, leaning closer to the blonde. "We could head over to the piano lounge. It's a bit darker and more private. The music should be starting up any minute now."

"I don't think so," the blonde said, pursing her puffy lips and rising to leave.

"At least take my card." The professor drew a business card from the pocket of his silk sport jacket and offered it to the woman. "Maybe we could meet somewhere on the Riverwalk later, for a nightcap."

"No thanks." The blonde drew a lipstick from her purse, narrowed her eyes at her reflection in the bar mirror, and retouched the thick coat of hot pink on her swollen lips. Then she walked off in the direction of the piano lounge.

The professor watched her go, squinting into the afternoon light reflecting up off the polished red-orange Spanish tile floor. When he turned back to face the bar mirror, he saw a dark-haired woman sit down on the stool vacated by the blonde.

"She did you a favor," the woman said, making eye contact with the professor in the bar mirror. "You can do better."

"Excuse me?"

"You can do better than the blonde. Talk about augmentation gone wild. Her lips looked like pink elephants."

The professor sipped his Guinness and looked away into the courtyard at the flames leaping from the basin of the signature Pat O'Brien's fiery fountain. Once darkness fell, a steady stream of tourists would have their waiters take pictures of them standing next to the flames that seemed to erupt from the water.

"Come on, don't get sore," the woman said. "We're both here for the same reason, aren't we?"

"Are we?" The professor looked back into the bar mirror, where he saw the dark-haired woman next to him signal the bartender.

"I'd like two Dulce Vida Tequila Añejos."

"Would you like them with water?" the bartender, a young woman with bright red hair pulled back into a ponytail and a white button-down shirt, asked.

"Just a splash." The bartender set the two glasses down in front of the dark-haired woman, who paid for the drinks and then slid one of the glasses toward the professor. "No hard feelings," she said. "I didn't mean any harm when I said her lips looked like pink elephants. I've got a pink elephant connection myself."

"Tequila and Guinness?" the professor said. "Are you kidding me?"

"Come on. Have you ever tried Dulce Vida Tequila Añejo? No? Then leave off the Guinness for a minute or two, and savor this."

"Look, I don't mean to be rude. But we shouldn't even be talking right now. And you know that."

"I know, I know," the dark-haired woman said. "But you're here. And I'm here. And it's happy hour. How about we agree not to even bring up... well, you know." She raised her glass toward the reflection of the professor in the bar mirror. "Let's make friends. How about another Hemingway reference? Will you please please please start talking?"

The professor grinned. "Do you know which collection Hemingway originally published 'Hills Like White Elephants' in?"

"No."

Men Without Women.

They both laughed, and the dark-haired woman slid her barstool a little closer to the professor. "You know," she said, "when they do a lip augmentation, the injection is either collagen from cow skin, or fat harvested from the belly or thighs of the injectee."

"Okay, so maybe you're right about me being better off without that particular woman."

"Let's drink to something," the dark-haired woman said. "What shall we drink to?"

"How about pink elephants?" They clinked their glasses together, and took slow sips of the tequila. In the bar mirror, the professor saw the woman smile.

"What do you think of the Dulce Vida?" she asked.

"At the risk of overdoing the Hemingway allusion, it tastes like liquorish."

"That's the way with everything," the woman said, and her smile disappeared. "Especially those things you've worked so hard, for so many years, to earn."

"I thought we agreed not to bring that up."

"You're right. It's just that...well, never mind." The dark-haired woman smiled brightly at the professor, as if to apologize. "You know, I really do have a pink elephant story. Would you like to hear it?"

"Sure." The professor sipped his tequila and turned to face the woman beside him.

"As a young girl," she began, "I was deprived of an imperative object: a pacifier. My father was against letting me have one. Luckily, though, for my first Christmas I received a stuffed elephant. I guess you could say this pacified me. Baby, as I originally named her, came to me dressed in a dainty pink dress along with a matching bow atop her head. She became my constant companion.

"I literally took her everywhere. As you can imagine, the years of wear and tear left Baby looking a bit tousled, just as any child's favorite toy. But to me, she was beautiful despite the smudges and tatters. Then one horrible night when I was visiting my grandparents' house, they took me to the local park with Baby in tow as usual. When we got back to their home, though, Baby was nowhere to be found. My grandfather went back to look, but had no luck. I was about as distraught as a four-year-old could be. The item in my life with the most emotional value was gone forever.

"Thankfully, a year before that, my parents had bought me a stuffed elephant almost identical to Baby. The only difference was that this elephant was a boy outfitted in green overalls. I dubbed him Other Baby, but I paid no attention to him because I was convinced he had cooties. After I lost my dear Baby, my grandmother had the idea to have Other Baby undergo a kind of sex change operation. She removed the overalls and created a beautiful pink dress almost identical to the original.

"At first, I was leery of the new, clean Baby. But as time passed, the new Baby slowly took the place of the old, and has been closely guarded ever since. She still holds more meaning for me than anything else I possess. Her numerous stitches, tatters, and tears represent more innocent

64

times. Every night when I get into bed, Baby is there watching over me. She always makes me smile when something really bad happens to me... like when I get denied some hugely important thing that I really deserve."

The professor, who had been smiling all through the story and sipping his tequila, suddenly frowned. He turned away from the woman and set his glass on the bar. "I appreciate the drink," he said, rising, "but I think I should go."

"Not without telling me why."

Instead of answering, the professor reached for his briefcase, which sat next to the barstool he'd just vacated. But as he turned to leave, he felt an uncomfortable pressure on his forearm. The dark-haired woman, he saw, had locked his navy sport jacket in a white-knuckled grip.

"Unhand me, madam," the professor said quietly but firmly.

"Not until you tell me why. If you don't start talking, I'll scream. And that's no Hemingway allusion."

"Go ahead and scream," the professor said. "I've done nothing wrong."

"That's not what I'll tell the police and the Provost. I'll tell them you tried to use your position on the committee to blackmail me for sex. And when I refused, you tried to force me. You've got a reputation as a shark, particularly among the female graduate students. And everyone in your department knows you come to happy hour at Pat O'Brien's to hit on tourists."

"Jeanette?" the professor called down the bar, taking care to keep his voice calm and even. "Would you bring us two more tequilas, please?"

The bartender came over to the corner of the bar where the dark-haired woman was sitting and the professor was standing. "You want them with water?"

"Would you like yours with water?" the professor calmly asked the dark-haired woman, who had not relaxed her grip on his arm.

"It's better with water."

"One with water," the professor said to the bartender, "one without." The bartender brought the drinks, and the professor shot his down all at once.

"I won't discuss the particulars," he said. "But I will agree to talk in general about the proceedings." He met the dark-haired woman's eyes that were wide, almost wild. "That is, if you'll agree to release my arm."

The dark-haired woman let go her grip and took a long, slow sip of tequila.

The professor paid for the drinks, set his briefcase back down next to the barstool, and took a seat. "What do you want to know?"

"I want to know why you voted no. I want to know why the committee voted no. I won the teaching award, for Christ's sake. How could I have been turned down?"

The professor sighed. "Look, it isn't about how well you teach. In essence, teaching is a side issue. It's about how much you publish, and where."

"I've got publications."

"A single book from a university press. And a few short stories. To put it simply, it's not enough."

"But what about all that service? What about all those great recommendation letters? Hell, I've got letters from major authors..." The dark-haired woman let her sentence trail off, downed the rest of her tequila, and signaled the bartender. "Could I get another one of these, please?"

"Make it two, Jeanette," the professor called. "The same as before."

"No," the dark-haired woman said. "This time, I'll pass on the water."

"Two more without water," the professor called. Then he turned back to the dark-haired woman, who had covered her eyes with one hand. "We are employed at a research institution," he said gently. "They don't want letters from major authors. They want a major author."

The bartender delivered the drinks, and the professor paid. Then he slid a glass of tequila over in front of the woman, who removed the hand from her face and downed the drink in a single gulp.

"It isn't fair," she said.

"Of course it's unfair. It's academe."

The dark-haired woman sat and stared into her empty glass.

"How about a pint of Guinness?" the professor asked gently. "This... what did you call it?"

"Dulce Vida Tequila Añejo."

"Right. Surprisingly, it goes pretty well with Irish beer. Jeanette, bring us a couple of pints of Guinness, please."

The bartender brought the pints, and the professor paid for them. Then he sat and sipped his Guinness, and saw the dark-haired woman do the same.

"You're right," she said. "High-octane Mexican tequila goes surprisingly well with Irish beer."

"You know, I have a pink elephant story of my own," the professor said. "It isn't a story that I share with very many people. But I think that, in this particular case, it might help. Would you like to hear it?"

"All right."

"My first full-time teaching job was at a community college. I got the job ABD, and spent two years teaching a 5/5 load and knocking out my dissertation. During that time, my now ex-wife and I had a daughter. We named her Catherine—my dissertation was on *A Farewell to Arms*—and we bought her a pink elephant for her first birthday. The elephant had a flower in its trunk, a daisy; and when Catherine was old enough to talk, she named it Horton after the elephant from *Horton Hears a Who.*

"I wish I could tell you whether the elephant was my daughter's constant companion. I wish I could tell you whether the elephant had more meaning for her than anything else she possessed. But the only thing I can tell you truthfully is about all of the nights and weekends I spent writing articles and books about a dead writer named Hemingway. I can tell you about all of the articles that I've published in the most prestigious journals, about all of the books I've brought out from the most distinguished academic presses, about how my work is in virtually every major library in the world.

"And I can tell you that when Catherine phoned me one Friday night, from the prestigious East Coast university I pressured her to go away to so that she could make a mark in life like her father, I was at a Hemingway conference in Italy...and I didn't take her call. She hanged herself in the restroom of her dormitory, at around 3 a.m. on that same Friday evening. Here is an inventory of all the fruits I've plucked as a result of thirty years of academic life: an endowed chair at a research university, a bunch of prestigious publications that maybe a hundred people will ever read, and a beat-up pink elephant with a daisy in its nose and stuffing coming out the seams."

"Is any of that true?" the dark-haired woman asked. "Or are you just trying to make me feel better?'

The professor, who had been looking out into the courtyard at the flames leaping from the water in the signature Pat O'Brien's fiery fountain, turned back to the woman beside him. "Actually, my ex-wife kept the elephant. But the rest is Gospel."

The dark-haired woman took a long pull off her pint of Guinness, and said nothing.

"I confess that I'm guilty of being a shark," the professor said after a long moment. "But I have never preyed on undergraduates. And I never even started on grad students until after my wife and I had split."

"I have a confession of my own," the dark-haired woman said. "I came here knowing that you argued against me at the meeting this morning. I came here with plans to pick you up, lure you back to my apartment, and kill you. Or else, if you wouldn't leave the bar with me, to raise a ruckus and accuse you of trying to force me. But after your pink elephant story, I think I've changed my mind...even though I do still sort of blame you for getting me fired."

"They're not going to fire you. Anyway, not yet. You've got the rest of this year, and all of next, to look for another job."

"I could also appeal the committee's verdict."

"That's certainly your right. And I wish you the best of luck, whichever path you choose," he said, rising to leave. "And now, if you'll excuse me, I believe I hear the music starting up in the piano lounge."

"If you strike out, feel free to come back and finish your beer."

The professor picked up his briefcase and carried it through the narrow patio and into the crisp, dark air of the piano lounge. He drank a Dulce Vida Tequila Añejo at the bar and looked at the blonde with the pink elephant lips, where she sat at a table drinking a hurricane with a man in a designer suit.

Then the professor went back out onto the patio. The dark-haired woman was still sitting at the bar, and she smiled reasonably at him.

"Did you strike out?" she asked.

"I never stepped into the batter's box. Still feel like doing me in?"

"I feel fine. I can't say there's nothing wrong with me," she said. "But right now, I feel fine."

I stared hard...
Tony Mares

thinking of Charles Bukowski

I stared hard at the hard-edged painting
    it was the sharp translucent line
    meant to be a glimpse at a micro-mini
    segment of the lace trim on a skirt
    wrapped around the gorgeous curves
    of a woman longing for me
    but inaccessible off the canvas
    at least I could imagine her

That's when I ordered my third tequila
    drank it straight like #s 1 & 2
    every woman at the bar glowed
    more beautiful than the ladies
    on a French postcard and shed
    ten years just like that too bad
    I am more aged than tequila *añejo*
    not that hard or sharp anymore

Christine Russell

Fifth Symphony
Gary Hawkins

The bottle, the shot glass, typical, ubiquitous, then empty,
the glass full again, the ubiquitous bottle,
the bottle—to hell with the glass,
the bottle the sun, my duskless bottle,
the bottle face-up, face-down, face-up, face-down in the swell,
the bottle washing up on land, a rustle in the dunes,
the bottle winking from the other side of the room,
the bottle with a high slit in its skirt,
the mouth of the bottle O'ing smoke rings that drift to the heavens,
this bottle is the body of Christ, which is for you,
this bottle of rust, bottle of tremor and dolor,
you can trust this bottle, or, this bottle will walk,
the bottle the whore, which is for you,
the bottle curled on the floor by the baseboard register,
the bottle encased in amber, unable to move,
the bottle, the bottle, the bottle,
a glass eye at the bottom of the bottle looking up at you,
the bottle curled by the baseboard register in the hall,
just rest right here, bottle, for another minute more,
the ubiquitous bottle, the bottle j'*adore*,
the bottle tangled in the branches of the tree in your backyard like a
    fallen moon.

What I Learned from the Fugitive's Mother
Robert Ashker Kraft

"It's interesting," I said. It was. The steaming plate of pasta in Marinara sauce in front of me was emitting a potent vapor of raw garlic, basil, and something that burned my eyes like turpentine fumes.

"Can you guess what I put in it?" she asked, gleefully.

I badly wanted to say "Turpentine?" but I thought she was beautiful and impish and I thought maybe I'd like to kiss her. And maybe marry her also.

"I can't tell," I said, rolling a pungent lump of pasta around my mouth in what I hoped was a gourmandly fashion.

"It's tequila! It's awesome. I'm a cooking genius!"

It really did taste like paint thinner. I think she must have just splashed half a pint into the sauce at the last minute and the alcohol hadn't had time to cook off. But it was also just a weird combination of flavors. She had used (bless her heart!) one of those jarred pre-made pasta sauces. "Now With More Basil!" said the jar. Tequila has that dark-but-light, musky sweetness that collided sharply with the tangy acidity of the tomato sauce and the sweetly savory notes of the "More Basil." Also, alcohol in cooking acts as a solvent, which creates liaisons between the different flavors in a dish, and allows potentially disparate flavors to meld together and become something new and, hopefully, better than the sum of their parts. In order for this alchemy to take place, the alcohol has to cook in the dish until it evaporates away, reducing down to the essential flavors of the wine, whiskey, beer—whatever is being used. Splashing the tequila in at the end of the process had made the dish nearly inedible. It is this kind of tricky, treacherous magic that attracted me to cooking in the first place.

I watched with dread as she retrieved the pan from the stovetop and slopped more of the fruits of her genius onto my pile of pasta. I wanted her to stop. But I was hoping there would be kissing. As it turns out, between the Malbec and the booze-laden spaghetti, I was buzzed enough to get up the nerve to kiss her neck as she leaned over me. It turned out to be the right thing to do.

But I did not, ultimately, marry her.

Her experiment got me thinking about cooking with tequila. I had used wine, of course, even beer, to deglaze pans, to make sauces, or just to lend richness to various sautéed dishes. But hard liquor was mostly used, as far as I knew, as a gimmicky glaze or sticky side-sauce for beef and chicken dishes at certain chain restaurants. Usually Bourbon, for some reason. But never as an accent ingredient in the dish, as attempted in this failed experiment.

Obviously, just because I haven't heard of something doesn't mean it's not out there. So I did a little research. Instead of getting in my truck and driving to the library or maybe a bookstore to pore over hundreds of cookbooks, as you would expect me to, I Googled "Cooking with Tequila" on my smart phone. I found lots of recipes, including Avocado Ice Cream, Caribbean Island Lime Shrimp, Margarita Balls, Margarita Wings, Margarita Pie, Margarita Shrimp Salad, a lot of recipes with Margarita in the name, Ribs with Mango Marinade, even Watercress Salad with Tequila Tangerine Dressing. Mostly recipes with a sweet-sour theme, with the tequila thrown in for show. I was looking for a real savory, as opposed to a sweet, or sour, or dessert application for the liquor.

I tried a few experiments with grilled meats, using tequila as part of the pre-grill marinade, with varying degrees of success. Nothing spectacular, but a few tasty successes. I discovered that of the varying types of tequilas, the Reposados seem to work best for cooking and reductions. The younger, lighter varieties—the Blancos, Silvers, or Platinums—are delicious for drinking, but since they haven't been alive as long, they have little aftertaste, or finish. It is the finish that you are left with when all the alcohol is cooked away; the woody accents acquired from months of resting in casks, and the complexity that develops from the continued mellowing of the agave sugars as the tequila sleeps. Aging imparts roundness and richness, a depth of character that blends well with savory spices like oregano and sage. So, basically, the older the tequila, the more it will bring to the process.

It is the sweetness of tequila that was problematic for me. The sugary top-notes make it difficult to work with in savory dishes. It is a problem child. Things cooled off with Spaghetti Girl, and I lost interest in the idea for a while.

A few months later I was out doing legwork for a fugitive-recovery case I was working on. I had sweet-talked my way into the home of the mother of the fugitive, and in my role as survey-taker, I was sitting at her kitchen table, sipping iced tea and discussing the War in Iraq. One of her sons was serving in Baghdad, and the other one was on the run for a gun charge, for which he had failed to appear. The bondsman who had bailed him out of jail was not happy, and that is how I ended up in her kitchen, pretending

73

to be taking an opinion survey on the War. The iced tea was very good, brewed in a one gallon jar in the sunlight on the windowsill. I felt dirty, like I always did, deceiving this woman in her own kitchen, accepting her hospitality, and secretly squeezing her for information about her fled son. We talked about the war, motherhood, and hard times. A pot of venison chili was simmering on the stovetop. A nephew had stopped by the day before with a haunch, needing room in his deep freeze for this summer's catch of crappie and white bass.

We talked a little bit about cooking. In the middle of our conversation, some internal clock alerted her, and she went to the cupboard and took down a bottle of molasses, and a bottle of maple syrup. While she told me about her younger son's promising teenage year—he had gotten into "trouble" some years ago, and had never gotten out and the promise seemed wasted now—she poured a few tablespoons of molasses and a splash of maple syrup into her venison chili, stirred the pot, covered it, and turned off the flame underneath.

"You put molasses and maple syrup into your chili?"

"Everybody does!"

"I don't in mine."

"Well, maybe you don't really make chili!" she sassed.

She said we had to wait for it to "melt together," then we could try a bowl. Half an hour later, I tasted it and I knew that she was right. I don't really make chili.

On my way back to the office, I thought of Spaghetti Girl, and I thought of tequila, and I thought about the sweetness problem. I wondered if tequila could find a home in the chili recipe I had extracted from the fugitive's mother. The only information I had managed to extract.

That night I pulled some venison out of the freezer, and the next day, I began to explore. The result was excellent. It wasn't as good as the fugitive's mother's chili, but it was different and it was good. Here is the recipe.

You will need: four pounds of chili-ground venison, or beef if you prefer; four large tomatoes; four bell peppers; two large onions; four or five large individual cloves of garlic; four or five good-sized jalapeno peppers; three or four habanero peppers.

Your dried seasonings will be: ground cumin, chili powder, cayenne pepper, oregano, basil, and of course, salt and pepper. You will also want a good strong Blackstrap Molasses, and, of course, a lovely dark reposado or anejo tequila.

Coarse chop the vegetables, except for the jalapenos and habaneros. What I mean by "coarse" is that it is okay to have large, half-inch chunks of the tomatoes, onions, and bell peppers, because the whole mess is going to cook for about eight hours, so you will want there to be some remnant of the vegetables in the final product for flavor and texture. If chopped too finely, they will just disappear into the meat. I start a fire under a pan, splash in some olive or canola oil, and do the onions and peppers first, throwing them into the pan as I chop. I do the tomatoes last, after the onions and peppers have softened. I season the vegetables while they are simmering with all of the spices mentioned above. I like to do this because it really saturates the vegetables with the flavors before they simmer in liquid later. Also because it smells delicious. Turn the fire under the vegetables down to medium.

Heat up another pan and oil it up. When the pan is good and hot, throw in the meat. You want a nice brown sear on all of the individual chunks. Season again with the cumin, chili powder, cayenne, oregano, basil, salt and pepper. Go easy with the cayenne in both pans, because you will be adding heat later with the jalepenos and habaneros. When the meat is nicely browned, pour in a shot or so of tequila. Let this reduce, then remove the meat from the fire. Let it rest while the vegetables simmer. After the onions have turned clear, and the peppers are dark green, throw the meat into the pan with the vegetables. Add water to the pot until it barely covers the mixture. You will have to keep doing this throughout the process to avoid burning on the bottom of the pan. Turn down the heat to a slow, gentle simmer. Peel the garlic cloves and toss them into the mix. Occasionally stir the chili throughout the entire process.

Simmer for five hours or so, seasoning as you go until you find the right balance between the cumin, basil, chili powder, and oregano. You will know it when you taste it. After five hours, turn off the heat and let the pot stand covered for a few hours on the stove. Put it in the refrigerator overnight.

The next morning return the pot to the fire, and let it simmer for a few more hours. The vegetables should be shimmering, gelatinous, and transparent. The connective tissue in the meat should all be melted away, and the meat should be soft and falling apart, almost a mush. In the final hour of simmering, dice up the habaneros and jalapenos, and add them. These are going to heat things up and add some characteristic flavors, so use sparingly and to taste. I suggest that you wear rubber gloves while handling the habaneros. Seriously. If you don't, avoid touching any part of your body, or anyone else's body, or petting your dog or cat for several days.

In the final half hour, add a tablespoon of Blackstrap Molasses and a cup or so of tequila. Let it all simmer for ten minutes or so, until all of the alcohol has cooked off, then cover the pot, turn off the heat and let stand. If there is still too much liquid in the pot, let it simmer uncovered until it the chili is a semi-solid.

Serve with Saltines, maybe some cheddar cheese on top. Share with friends. Take containers of chili to your favorite bartender, or the guy that fixes your car. Build a fire in your chiminea and invite friends over for beer and chili. Eat the chili outside under a tree, with stars glancing through the branches, and the wind whispering in the leaves. Tell everyone that it was made with tequila, and that you are a cooking genius. Thank the fugitive's mother.

Bacardi Margarita
Antonia Murguia

Quiero una margarita
A sentir el amor de la música.
On the rocks
With a little salt around the edges
To enhance the taste,
Made with Bacardi Silver,
The good stuff that goes down smooth.

Quiero una margarita
A sentir el amor de la música.
I want to feel the energy of each song.
I want the rhythm to enter my soul.
I want to be margarita happy.

Quiero una margarita
A sentir el amor de la música.
Margarita, margarita,
Sabor frío y delicioso,
Dame otra!

> (I want a margarita
> to feel the love of the music.
> Cold taste and delicious
> Give me another)

Antonia's Margarita Recipe
1 can Frozen Bacardi Margarita Mix
5 ounces of Bacardi Rum
½ blender of crushed ice
Salt
1 lime

Take a slice of lime and rub around the rim of your favorite margarita glass. Dip glass rim in salt. Fill ½ of blender with crushed ice. Pour a can of frozen Bacardi Margarita Mix and 5 ounces of Bacardi Rum into blender. Blend until liquefied and pour into margarita glass. Enjoy!

Diving into Love
Jerry Bradley

you stand on the rail
dreaming what will happen
when you bottom in the shallows
strangling on your necklace of stars

how the drop will crack you
like adobe where the HazMat team
waits on the rocks
to gather your remains

you fear what your heart has to say
what will happen if you fall
back into yourself

what will happen
if you don't

and licking the salt from your palms
you cross your fingers
like you do at bingo
and plunge

hoping to be lucky
if only for tonight
when you open the motel door

but already knowing
how the tequila bites
just like a South Valley girl

Five Easy Margaritas
Sherry Craven

I.
With the first one, strawberry, I think, frosty-iced and
nestled into the mug, he said I was just about the prettiest,
then we ordered another, no strawberry this time,
straight, no rocks, and I ripened beyond prettiest.

The second margarita brought out his astrological knowledge,
which it seems was limited to my sign, Sagittarius, which,
 it turns out was his, too. What luck. I was most interesting.

The third margarita brought him closer, hot breath melting
cold ice, lime-scented ideas pouring, salt-flavored longings.
I was beautiful, positively glowing, filtered through margarita magic.

The room spun on the axis of the fourth drink,
tequila the boss now, el jefe , my lover, my child, and my
new best friend all at once. Helluva deal. I was his blue
agave princess, Aztec and volcanic all at once.

II.
Somewhere in the midst of the fifth margarita, I lost the passion-ride,
felt my features slide around my face, mouth move south, eyes north,
and upon tequila self-scrutiny, I misplaced myself.

When the sixth the came, I had slipped back before pretty, ready
to be thrown from the pyramid of the sun, surrender into *nada*,
jelly legs and a quicksand bar floor my support. His astrological

knowledge had left him, which was my saviour because a benevolent
booze-clarity took hold while he was looking at his watch and the girl
at the next table, and I called a cab to take me on a ride
home. Alone.

Old Man
Robert Whitsitt

Remember when you were going to a dinner party and were quite nervous, so you drank a quick glass of tequila (blue agave, of course) before you left home? Well, maybe not; you're probably more responsible than that. But when you got to the party and they were serving yummy snacks and glasses of French champagne, you had one, and then a second, right? Just to calm yourself, to get in the mood. Then dinner started with a crisp clear *Pinot gris* to accompany the rich, brown mushroom soup. And it would be impolite not to have a couple of glasses—they weren't all that big anyway—of a gorgeous cabernet with the Chateaubriand (the original Julia Child recipe!) the host had slaved over. Remember?

By that time you were totally clueless about the names of the new people at the party. In fact, some of the people you actually knew well, you couldn't always come up with their names quickly. But you could smile, and laugh when the others laughed, so it was okay, pretty much.

After dinner you joined them in sipping glasses—how many?—of tawny port, and they turned to discussing events of the day, who won the lottery, the week's 3D shows, the latest political scandal. Things you had maybe heard of but never really understood. Maybe you followed things like that at one time, but you didn't really remember. You tried to follow the discussion, and maybe had something to say but the conversation was so fast! By the time you could get a sentence together the time was gone, so you sat there feeling dumb. Friendless. Alone in a crowd of chattering, engaged, lively people.

Remember? Remember feeling confused and helpless and hopeless and sad and frustrated and worthless, at least for that time?

That's how the old man felt all the time.

* * *

The old man sat in the right seat, a youngish woman in the left. Who was she? Oh, yes, Abril. They were going to see... a doctor?

Abril glanced at the console. "It says we'll be there in eight minutes, Gramps."

Abril. Yes, his, hmm. His granddaughter's daughter. "Okay." Then tentatively, "Where?"

Abril never displayed any pique. "The rejuve clinic. Your intake interview. Remember?"

After much thought, "Yes, I remember now. Thank you for reminding me. Abril."

She looked at him and smiled. "You're welcome, Gramps."

* * *

The office felt more like it belonged to a lawyer than a doctor, rich mahogany and high ceilings. The old man and Abril sat in two identical leather chairs across an empty desk from a man sitting comfortably in a black high-backed stuffed chair. The doctor, wearing a conservative business suit, rocked back and forth an inch or so as he spoke.

The old man sat hunched over, his eyes on the dark green carpet with flecks of brown that matched the wood on the walls.

The doctor said carefully, "Here's my first question. You're name is James, right?"

"Jimmy, actually."

Abril said, "Now, Gramps."

"Oh, right. These days my real name means oral sex. Okay, I'm James."

The doctor peered at him, then opened what the old man thought of as a laptop and stared at it. "You were born in the year 2000. What date?"

"January 11."

The doctor nodded. "You have applied for rejuve treatment. Why?"

The old man thought a moment. "I've had a good life. A wonderful first marriage and a completely... satisfactory second. I raised three children and now have grandchildren and greatgrandchildren... and even more." The old man looked over at Abril. "Where was I?"

Abril smiled at him.

After a moment he went on, "But lately I don't feel so good. I can't remember things, and I ache, and I don't know what's going on... in the world. Very depressing." The old man looked up at the doctor. "And then I heard more and more about rejuve. I want to go back. To have a memory again. Yes. To feel good. To know... stuff. To be with people. You know?"

The doctor waited. When nothing more was forthcoming, he said, "I know. But you need to understand that what we can do is make you feel young again. Getting back into the real and virt worlds, getting reacquainted, making a new life, finding a new partner: those are harder. You'll get guidance and support, but you'll have to do it yourself. Work at it. Do you think you can do that?"

The old man nodded.

"Okay. We'll go on. Where did you go to high school?"

"Carmel High, Indiana. The Greyhounds."

"College?"

"Umm, let me think. A. Moment. Please.... Ah. Kent State undergraduate, then Temple and Stanford. Didn't finish my Ph.D."

"Married?"

"Twice. Second wife died 15 years ago. I'm alone now."

"You live alone?"

"I'm in a retire home with lots of strangers. I guess that means I'm not alone."

The doctor leaned back and looked at the old man. He scratched his temple, glanced at Abril and then back at the old man. "Okay, James, I think it's worth going to the next step. Let me tell you how this works. Interrupt any time.

"Over the next week or so I want you to tell your companion some of the highlights of your life. I'll give you an app to help the process. You don't have to tell every detail, just highlights. Whatever comes into your mind. The point is to see what you remember. Like all elderly people you have a retrieval deficit." He blinked. "That is, you can't pull memories back quickly. The questions we need to answer before we proceed are: One, if the memories are in there, just difficult to retrieve. And two, if you are making new memories.

"We're almost done. Do you have any questions?"

"I had my appendix removed when I was 48. Will it grow back when you do the thing?"

The doctor nodded. "Good question. At the end of the first part of the procedure everything will be back where it was when you were about 35. But we have your medical records, so in the final steps we'll remove your appendix, strengthen your rotator cuffs, and do several other procedures to deal with areas that gave you trouble one time or another over your healthspan. That is, your healthspan so far. We'll also lessen your fears of public speaking and heights, but not so much that it changes who you are. We've been doing this for nearly 45 years and are pretty good at it. I think you're a very good candidate.

"I should mention the cost. As you've probably heard, you pay for this procedure by returning to work for 50 years before you retire again and go back on security. For someone your age, that's no time at all. And a good trade for being young again, right?"

The old man continued to look at the floor.

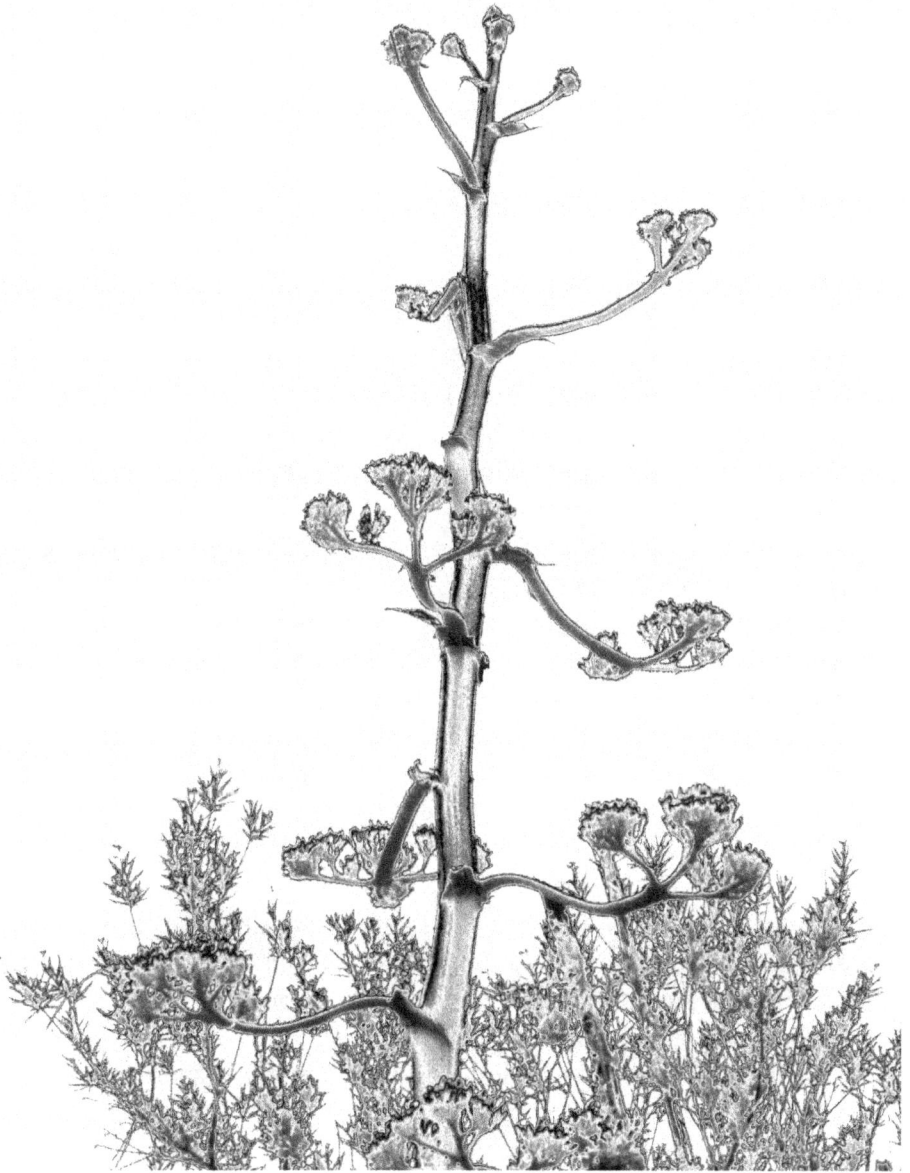

Terry Dalrymple

After a moment the doctor said, "Do you have any other questions for me?"

The old man shook his head slowly.

"Here's a pamphlet that has all of the information you need. Your companion can help you with it."

"Dog."

The doctor looked at Abril. "Dog?"

Abril whispered, "His companion is a dog."

The doctor said, "Not a person? Interesting." He looked back at the old man. "Very well, then. As I said, we need to know if you are making new memories. So, tell me: What was the first question I asked you today?"

The old man looked up at the doctor, then back down at the carpet. While he'd been paying good attention, as good as his attention ever was now, the flow of the conversation was not always with him. Seconds went by. First question? Hmm. He glanced at Abril, who looked quickly away, then back at him. "Gramps?"

The doctor wasn't rocking anymore, just quietly waiting, looking at a picture on the wall. No pressure.

The old man smiled at Abril. Maybe that would help. If only. Ah! "First question: 'Your name is James?' Then we talked about what the diminutive of my name has come to mean. I did, anyway."

The doctor grinned. "Excellent, James. I'll let Abril set you up at home. Here's the memory." He handed Abril a small silver disk about a centimeter thick. "It has all the instructions so you can set it up, Abril. He does have full computer use, doesn't he?"

"Yes, doctor. Thank you so much!"

The old man got up from the chair, a major undertaking, and started toward the door. Abril came beside him and took his arm. She said quietly, "I'm so excited! Are you excited? They can put you back where you were a hundred years ago, a puppy again!"

The old man stopped and looked up at her. He turned around and looked at the doctor. "Less if I pay more taxes, right?"

The doctor said, "What? Excuse me?"

"You know. If I pay lots of taxes, then it's less."

The doctor looked at Abril. "Do you know what he's talking about?"

The old man said, a little too loudly, "Taxes. If I pay taxes then... Oh, the 50 years. I don't have to work it all. Right?"

The doctor said, "Oh, quite right, James. If you pay a large amount of taxes then you won't have to work the entire 50 years before you retire again. But the amount of taxes to reduce the time is quite large, and most people will end up working the entire 50 years."

"Thank you." The old man turned again and walked toward the door.

Abril stood a moment and then caught up with him, again taking his arm. "That was great, Gramps! How did you know to ask that?"

"You only see me a few hours a week. I read stuff on the, um, net. There's a lot of stuff about rejuve. I've been reading about it for decades.

"Which reminds me, Maryjane, give me the disk thing, memory thing. I can set up my own interview app. Me and Dog."

Abril got the memory out. "Are you sure?"

"Abril, I was... I just called you Maryjane, didn't I? Have I told you how much you're like her? I mean how you're like she was to me. Nice. Friendly. Supportive. You don't look like her, though. She had light brown hair and light skin and sort of green eyes. Your hair is black and shiny, your eyes dark brown, and your skin kind of medium brown." He stopped and looked at her. "She was prettier, but not much. Or maybe I'm not remembering her right.... Anyway, I was a programmer at, you know, Google? And other places. That means, um, I can easily deal with anything that has to do with today's apps. I can install this. Me and Dog."

Abril handed the memory to him. "Call me if you need me."

"Hmph."

Back in the car they rode in silence for a few minutes.

"Where are we going now, Maryjane?"

"Back to your home."

"Okay. Remind me where that is?"

"Willows. On Telegraph. In Oakland. That's in California, Gramps. You don't remember?"

It was easier to agree. "Oh. Right." He lived in California? How the heck did he get way out West? Why not in Cleveland?

* * *

The old man went into his study, which was a lot of books—some of them very old—on all four walls. No windows, but a full-spectrum light that changed its hue and brightness according to the season and time of day. Displayed on the two-meter 3D on one wall was a Labrador Retriever curled up, snoring gently.

"I'm back! Wake up, you silly mutt."

The dog looked at him. "Hi, Jimmy. I was dreaming about you."

"I bet you were. I have an interview app to install."

"Is this about rejuve?"

"Yep. I'm considering doing it."

"Okay, put the memory in the slot. No, that's upside down. Wait a minute. Hmm. Yep, I can install it for you. Oh, wait. I need your permission to give my entire memory to the app."

"Okay. What? My entire, I mean, your entire memory, Dog? Not just relevant parts?"

"Because it is medical, the app doesn't know which parts of my memory are relevant, so it wants all of it. This is going to take a while, Jimmy, so don't get impatient. Want to play a game while you wait for this to set up? Checkers? Syzygy? Lexicose?"

* * *

[Transcript of conversations with James Allen Newsome pursuant to full rejuvenation appropriateness analysis.

Conversations selected based on the app's instructions to analyze James' ability to recall old memories and retain new memories.

On advice of James' companion, pauses longer than 30 seconds are indicated. There are many pauses of fewer than 30 seconds.

The companion indicated that James should be interrupted after a pause of more than a minute, as his thoughts likely have strayed to another topic.

Semantically null sounds such as "um" and "er" and "uh" removed for clarity.

No linguistic analysis applied to improve the communication, so other than as described above, these are James' words.]

You listening, Dog?

I'm listening.

Okay.

[Break of 43 seconds.]

I don't really remember all that much about my childhood. At the time it was all-consuming and terribly significant, but after more than a century it doesn't mean much.

[Break of 32 seconds.]

Oh, I remember something. Samantha Nyburg. She was one of the eleven girls in the advanced math class in tenth grade. She was a mousy little thing, dark hair, always wearing dark or gray or beige clothing. A prototypical wallflower. She sat behind me when the teachers arranged us alphabetically, but in math class she was in front of me. I guess the math teacher didn't care about the alphabet. He sure cared about geometry, though! I thought it was dumb. Even after my degrees in math, I thought it was dumb.

Anyway, Samantha, who the teacher called Sam to her obvious discomfort, was always quiet. The teacher kept calling on her, though. She knew her stuff. I spoke to her a couple of times in the first month, and then regularly. She was cute and quiet and nice and all the good things like that, but a social recluse. I had a crush on her, and I like to think she kind of liked me. We could talk comfortably, which was not a skill I usually had at that time.

The next year, eleventh grade, when I walked into math class the boys were all gathered around where my alphabetical seat would put me. I pushed my way through and then stopped and stared. Samantha was in a crimson blouse, low cut, with a short sky blue skirt, orange knee socks, and lime green tennis shoes. Her hair was all combed to one side and had magenta and green streaks in it. OMG!

Class started and Samantha didn't have to be called on. She volunteered. She chatted with the teacher and flirted with the boys. She was friends with the girls. I couldn't believe it.

In the cafetorium during lunch Samantha came over to my corner and sat beside me. I smiled at her and she smiled back. "How you doing, Jimmy?"

"Fine." I looked at her, up and down, which made her smile. I said, "What happened?"

She knew what I was talking about. "I looked around at what was going on in the world and realized that I was missing out on things. Lots of things. I thought I'd try being different. I did a google on makeup and dress and how to talk with people, which mostly means active listening. You know. During the summer we went to Berkeley for Mom and Dad to do some research, and I tried out different ways of being me. This way got me the most friends of the right kind. Mostly the right kind." She hesitated. "It kind of overdoes the boy attraction thing, though. I think I'll tone that down."

She looked at me intensely. "You're not the kind of boy that talks easily to what I'm pretending to be, Jimmy. Or what I'm becoming, maybe. But you're the kind of guy I like. Want to go to the dance Friday?"

So we did. We dated a few more times, but even though she cut back a little on the bright colors and raised her neckline, she was way out of my league.

In a novel, Samantha and I would get back together in a clever romantic twist. In reality, though, I used the net to follow her distinguished career as a math professor until she died in 2086. We never spoke again after high school.

[Break of more than a minute.]

Are you okay?

I'm fine, Dog. We're done for now.

* * *

I should tell you about 2085. It's much on my mind since I have to be thinking about the past. September 19, 2085.

Well.

[Break of more than a minute.]

Are you okay?

Shut up.

[Break of more than a minute.]

I know that you told me to be quiet, but I have to ask if you are okay because you're crying. Are you in pain? Do you need a doctor?

I'm fine. This session is over.

* * *

You recording, Dog?

Yes. You don't have to ask me that. I'm paying attention.

Whatever.

Maryjane and I were married November 17, 2018. I was almost 19, she had just turned 21. We met at Kent State University in my sophomore year. She hated her home life, and I wasn't too happy with mine (I guess we were pretty typical for our age) and running away together made sense to us. We were married in Michigan. I think Michigan. She wasn't my first girlfriend, since I did quite well in that department after Samantha and I stopped dating. Did I tell you about Samantha?

Yes.

Maryjane was very social outwardly, while being quietly attentive to me. It was wonderful! Our marriage was in a courthouse with no one but the judge. From there we went to Philadelphia. First I finished my undergraduate degree and then started teaching math. Then she went through with her masters in library science. Then I went back for my masters. We took turns.

I don't know how to tell you how good our marriage was. We rarely argued, we agreed on everything, or nearly.

We got pregnant around mid-September 2021. Money was tight and we didn't really want to. Maryjane was frantic! She was terrified of carrying the baby to term, terrified of being a mother, terrified by our financial situation. I tried to calm her, but she cried and cried over the first three months. Finally, late one tearful night, I said, "This isn't worth it. You want an abortion, go get one. Then we'll never talk about it again."

She looked at me and said, "Are you out of your mind! Of course I want this baby!" And she never cried or complained about it again.

I'm tired now, Dog. I'll tell you about the baby later.

* * *

That was weird. Abril—You know who that is?

Yes, your greatgranddaughter.

Yes. Abril was taking me to the grocery. As we came out I noticed an odd-looking guy. His face was young like a puppy, sort of, but in a kind of plastic weird way, like a facelift gone wrong. His forearms were tiny, with the slightest muscle and skin pulled tight over the bones, and he walked with tiny steps like an elderly man. But he seemed to have plenty of energy.

The guy came over and said to me, "Hey, old man! Don't do it, man! It's awful! They say it'll be like when you were 35, but it isn't. It's weird, man. I was one of the first, born 1983, rejuve 2090. It's been hell, man. Don't do it! All my life has been like that, you know? It's bad, man."

I walked past him and let Abril guide me toward the car. Abril said, "Are you okay, Gramps?"

"I'm fine. People don't change all that much. I'd bet good money that guy was negative and irritating all his life. He's, what, 152 years old? He was always a nut and he still is. Nothing to do with me."

Abril stopped and looked at me. "You've been talking to the computer, haven't you. About old memories."

"Yep, and that's got the juices flowing. At least a bit. Did I ever tell you about Samantha?"

We got in the car and I told her. She said she thought she knew all my stories, and was glad to hear a new one. Maryjane used to say that. Although most of my stories were with her, so I rarely had anything new to tell her.

I'd like to talk to Maryjane about that weird puppy old man.
[Break of 51 seconds.]

That wasn't about the past, at least not exactly. I hope it isn't wrong to tell you that.

It's fine.
Okay then.

* * *

Saffny was born on June 5, 2022. She was a perfect baby and a perfect person. Well, in retrospect, anyway. There were the usual issues with toilet training, drug use, one abortion ("And there better not be another, young lady: use contraception!"), drinking, and that sort of stuff, but nothing unusual.

Teaching was rewarding in many ways, but frustrating, too. In 2025 after the school year ended, Maryjane and I moved us and Saffny to Cleveland, Ohio. With its active high-tech community we figured we could fit in. I'd learned how to program as an undergraduate and Maryjane as a librarian would always be in demand to keep track of the world's information. We found jobs at a startup and learned how demanding that was. And there was no longer a summer vacation! What was up with that?

Still, the pay was more that double what we got teaching, and we decided to have a second child. Hailey was born October 14, 2026. As with Saffny we had no unusual troubles with her. They both turned in to great people. Thinking of them makes me smile.

[Break of 34 seconds.]

So, we worked for half a dozen high-tech companies in Cleveland. Two went public. The first one gave us enough to put all three of our kids through college. The second one let us retire when we were only 70! That was really good. Travel and plays and volunteer work—Maryjane more than me. We did that for...

[Break of more than a minute.]

Are you okay?

I'm thinking about September 19, 2085. Damn.

Damn. Damn. Damn.

Look, I know this is important, Dog—Abril—I mean, Doctor. Look, I know I'm really talking to you when I'm doing this, Doctor. I want to live again, I want to be like it, well, like it was. But with new people, since I can't have the old people.

Damn.

I'm done. Later. Dog, turn the 3D to *Buffy*. The musical one. You know.

* * *

Jayden was born May 17, 2030. He was our last. He had more problems than the girls, with wild teen years: a couple of arrests for drunk driving and one slash fight. He won by disabling the other kid, not actually hurting him much. Saffny and Hailey took him aside one Friday evening when he was 19 and was about to go out with his friends. They shouted. All three of them. Maryjane and I stayed out of it, and after a while the three of them went out. They didn't come home that night. In the morning I called Saffny's cell. She said they were all three fine, and they'd be home soon. Maybe in a few days.

I called again four days later. Saffny sounded exhausted. She said all was well. That we should wait.

They came home eight days after they left. They all smelled of sweat and booze and something I never identified. Yucky. They took showers and then said they wanted to go out to a good dinner. We went to Swansen's and had natural filet mignon. All three of them were subdued, Jayden the most. Everyone but Jayden had wine with dinner, all a reasonable amount. I never saw Jayden drink again.

I wish I knew what happened those eight days they were gone. At least I think I do. I asked all three of them at one time or another, as did Maryjane. All of the kids gave us some version of "you don't want to know." We'd say, "Yes, we really do want to know." And they said, "No. You really don't."

Dog, any guesses what happened those eight days?

They all got very drunk and sick, like giving a ten-year-old a cigarette to make her hate it?

Hmm. Could be. Doesn't quite work, though.

* * *

All my children are dead. Saffny lived to be 85, Hailey to be only 30, killed in a car crash. A drunk ran a red light. I can't believe shit like that still happens!

[Break of 38 seconds.]

Jayden, our youngest, lived to be only 69. He wore out. Strange that our kids didn't live all that long since I'm still alive and kicking at 135, and Maryjane lived to be 85. That's a ripe old age, right? She died on September 19, 2085, after we were married for nearly 67 years. But I don't want to talk about that, Dog. Screw that.

* * *

91

Okay, I'm back. Here's something else that the good doctor might find interesting while he's busy roiling my mind in the past that might best be forgotten.

I met Kathryn in 2088. She was only 68 to my 88, but I was a good strong 88. We were at a party and the hostess sat us next to each other. We were the oldest there, she by a few years, me by a couple of decades. We flirted and carried on and I had the most fun since Maryjane had died three years earlier.

Kathryn wasn't like Maryjane. She was happy-go-lucky and make-the-sparks. She would do all sorts of wild things, some of which made me uncomfortable: skinny dipping in a park fountain; making love in a restaurant toilet; kissing a passing man in uniform and then winking at him and walking on, her arm through my arm, her cheek against my shoulder, laughing quietly to herself. She introduced me to tequila, and taught me how important it was that it was made only from the blue agave. It remains my quick drink of choice. And, actually, my sipping drink, too.

We married in 2093. By then Saffny was 71 and kind of a stick in the mud who totally didn't approve. Hailey had been dead for 37 years. Jayden, who was just 63, thought Kathryn was a hoot. Sometimes they'd go off on their own expeditions doing god knows what, having a great time!

Kathryn died in 2120 after we'd been married 27 years. It was a brief time, but excellent. She was wild and crazy to the end. When she turned 100 she told me that she was done, ready to end it. "It's been a fantastic century, but I don't think I have that much more in me." She was contemplating suicide and how to do it, over my objections, when she got an aggressive cancer they couldn't deal with and died in a couple of months. She grinned at me on her deathbed and winked just before she died. "I can't wait to hear who you marry next!" were her last words to me.

I miss her. She was a great friend and companion, and I really loved her.

[Break of 49 seconds.]

But she wasn't Maryjane.

* * *

Okay, some genealogy, Doctor. Saffny's daughter Belinda was born in 2052. In the spring, I think. She's 87 and in quite good health. She's considering rejuve in the next decade or two. Her daughter, Abril, was born in 2080, so she's a vibrant young woman of 55. She's my

92

greatgranddaughter, and takes excellent care of me. She visits me and takes me places. Not just shopping, but plays and museums. Concerts sometimes. I really love her. Her son, Rajeev, was born in 2113, so he's a puppy, only 22 years old and still in school.

From all of this, Doctor, I'm sure it is obvious that I am physically and intellectually a good candidate for rejuve. I have to wonder, though, if I am emotionally equipped for another 100 years. Of late I'm sometimes weepy, especially when I think of Maryjane who has, after all, been dead for 50 years, and was my wife before last. Why should I care so much?

[Break of more than a minute.]

Are you okay James?

I'm crying, you stupid machine. Shut up, Dog.

[Break of more than a minute.]

Excuse me for interrupting, but you're still crying.

Yes, I know that. Not good, huh?

Oh, it's okay. I thought you might want to tell me why.

Why do you think?

You miss Maryjane, and you fear that the memory of her will always cause you pain.

[Break of 31 seconds.]

You know, that's interesting. On the one hand, you're exactly right. I miss her, and I always will though it's been 50 years. I suspect I still will miss her after 150 years. If I decide to keep going. Living. On the other hand, she's also a critical part of the best years of my life. Without her, would I have ever gone to Cozumel or New Zealand or the Galapagos, or have spent a thousand euros for the dinner of our life at *La Tour d'Argent* in Paris for our 50th anniversary? The memory of her is in large part a memory of me at my best! That's part of what she gave me.

But the loss of her is so hard, Dog. So hard.

So hard.

[Break of 54 seconds.]

I can't go on like I am now, like I have been for the last 20 or 30 years. I need to live again... or I need to die. Not this half life, Dog.

Do you think I've given enough so the doctor can evaluate me?

I've sent transcripts to the doctor as they occurred. He has made a tentative decision, but he would like to hear about September 19, 2085.

Damn him. I'll be back later.

* * *

First, Doctor, let me say that what I've done the last few days has been useful to me, even if you turn me down. I've reminded myself of how good—how very good—life can be. How much I enjoyed it, before. There are the bad things of course. But the good things outweigh them, I think. Anyway, here's what you asked for, Doctor.

September 19, 2085. It actually started a couple of weeks earlier. Maryjane had pneumonia and we took her to the emergency room. It turned out that she also had something they called sepsis syndrome, which meant that she was infected all over her body. While they treated that, she picked up one of those nasty bugs that only exist in hospitals, so they had to treat her for that.

It was awful. She was, strangely, not in much pain, but she was in and out of consciousness. She told me over and over how much she loved me, and always would.

The morning of September 19 I went in as usual. She was sitting up in bed. She had a little makeup on and looked quite good, not the way she had for days and days. I grabbed her and held her close. I so wanted to believe.

She explained that she wanted to be that way as a surprise. They told her that her body wouldn't last more than a few days, but that they could give her a drug cocktail that would let her be near normal for a few hours. Then, of course, she would die quickly from the stress.

Well, I guess she had a right to her decision, although it has haunted me. For a couple of hours we talked and bantered and relived the memories of all the places we had been and the people we had known. We laughed a lot. Then she said she was tired. Very tired. I called the nurse and he lowered the bed to be flat and told me it was likely a few minutes.

I leaned close to Maryjane and said, "Thank you so much my darling. I will love you forever."

She kept her eyes closed, but said, "James, my one and only. So good."

And she died.

[Break of more than a minute.]

I've sent this to the doctor. He'd like you to come in tomorrow.

Okay, Dog. Would you ask what's-her-name, Abril, to set up an appointment?

Certainly.

* * *

The old man waited while Abril told the car where to take them.

"Are you okay, Gramps? You were talkative this last week while you did your work for the doctor. But you've been quiet today."

"Yep."

"Dollar for your thoughts?"

"Inflation's a bitch."

"Gramps?"

"Is this a good idea? I've had a great life. A hundred and thirty-five years! Do I need more? Do I deserve more?"

"Most of the time you seem to think so. I think you'll love being young again! Anyway, what would I do without you?"

"Get a life. Get away for a month at a time. Don't always be tied to me."

"Gramps, you know I don't think of taking care of you as a burden. I'm happy to do it!"

"Yes, I know. But am I happy to have you need to do it?"

* * *

The doctor's office hadn't changed. The doctor smiled at the old man.

"I'll come right to the point, James. We believe you're an excellent candidate for rejuve. Barring any mishaps, the treatment should take approximately six months. During that period you will be sedated much of the time, so it will only feel like a couple of months to you. Are you excited?"

"I'm having second thoughts."

"About the 50 years of required work? No? About how you'll feel? No? Then, what?"

"What do I do to find another love of my life? Where can I find another Maryjane?"

"Oh, come on, James. You'll be effectively 35, a puppy again. You have your choice of friends and lovers and partners. It'll be great. Here's the document to sign."

He put the paper in front of the old man and handed him a pen. James looked at the paper. Read the few words quickly. "I just don't know."

Abril said, "Of course you don't have to, Gramps, but I think it would be a good idea. You like to live! I've seen you!"

The old man said, "I do at that. My life has been very shiny. But I'm not sure I want to go on another hundred years, and maybe hundreds and hundreds after that. I'm really not sure. Just not sure."

The old man sat, looking at the paper, pen in hand.

Terry Dalrymple

The Second One
Sandra Soli

Never accept a third Tequila Sunrise, and look at the second one with suspicion. One memorable summer evening in Darmstadt, a deeply upholstered couch invited relaxation in congenial company and the glow of my first Tequila Sunrise. It was the second one that got me. Even in pointed-toe heels and a state of euphoria, I managed to rise from the sofa just fine; and, having scoped out the nearest route to the guest bathroom, floated to the floor.

Classic Tequila Sunrise Recipe

For each drink:
Ice cubes, the pretty square ones
1 jigger Tequila (1 oz.)
Cup orange juice
2 Teaspoons lime juice
1-2 Tablespoons grenadine syrup
Orange twist for garnish
Maraschino cherry for garnish

Place ice cubes in tall glass. Add Tequila, OJ and lime juice. Stir to just mix with an iced tea spoon. Slowly add grenadine on the top. Do not stir. Garnish with an orange twist and cherry. Alternative: Mix enough for 6 drinks in a pitcher except for grenadine and add that to taste at the end, depending on how sweet people like their drinks. To make orange twist: cut thin orange slices and remove any seeds.

Cut a slit in each slice just to the center. Twist the cut edges in opposite directions and place on top of drink or perch the slice on side of glass.

La Señorita Margarita
Scott Wiggerman

I have savored you,
a perfect blend
of provocative tastes:
sweet with triple sec,
sour as fresh-cut lime,
bitter as its ghostly pith,
salty like the glass's rim.

I have swallowed
the froth of pleasure,
licked the iciness
away from your lips.

Daring like the curl of worm
at the bottom of a bottle,
intoxicating as you are,
I have learned to stop
when I've had enough.

Redbird, Tequila and Me
Cindy Jordan

Tequila
The word makes people smile
Why?
Tequila means freedom from our mind
"Take another shot of courage"
"Tequila makes your clothes fall off"
Like a toddler who rips off her diaper and runs through the sprinkler
Joyful!
Laughing with glee!
As the Divine watches through her eyes
See the world as a little child
You will see the Kingdom of Heaven
I have a friend with flaming red hair that looks like fire in the sun
I call my friend "Redbird"
Redbird and I were at a party
The hot tub looked so inviting
We didn't have swim suits
No problem... We had tequila!
The water was warm
Our breasts floated in the bubbles
Redbird and I were laughing with glee!
Joyful!
Like the toddler running through the sprinkler
Freedom!
Both of us grandmothers
I guess we forgot
Redbird and I were out of our minds
Joyful freedom!
This is good for the soul
A Divine witness watched through our eyes
A wonderful memory
Will we do it again?
Probably not
Yes tequila gives you courage
Yes tequila makes your clothes fall off
Now when Redbird say the word, *tequila*
We giggle
A lot!

Norte Americanos

R Dean Johnson

Two guys with shaved heads and Scotland jerseys get on the tram one stop after me. One of them is carrying a six-pack of beer, and as soon as we're moving again he pops open a can and hands it to his friend, then pops one open for himself. At the next stop, as the tram fills past capacity, these guys slide over near me, the one with the six-pack hugging a pole with the arm that's only holding one beer. There's an older guy, gray hair and weathered face, who is right next to us, looking the Scottish guys up and down. "Glasgow Celtic?" he says in a thick brogue.

"Aye, Celtic," the one with the six-pack says, matching the old Scot's brogue and holding up his beer for an imaginary toast.

The old Scot shakes him off. "Rangers," he says, dipping his chin to claim what that means. And what it means isn't just that Rangers and Celtic are rival soccer teams from the same city, Glasgow. For as long as it has mattered, Rangers have been the Protestant team while Celtic have been the Catholic team. Team loyalty, therefore, goes to their very souls. "Aye," the one with the six-pack says again, undeterred and raising his beer for another imaginary toast. "But while we're here, we're all Scotsmen."

The old Scot agrees and is given a beer to confirm the temporary truce.

The young Scot hands a second beer to his friend and takes out a second for himself. Then he turns to me, one beer left in the six-pack. "You want a beer?"

"Sure," I say. "Thanks."

"American?" he says. "What are you doing here?"

The long answer is that I'm trying to find the tourist office, hoping they can help me find a place to stay. I give him the short answer: "Same as you. Football."

"Hey!" he and his friend cheer. Even the old guy gives me a grin.

For the better part of two weeks, I've been the rarest of things in Europe: a beloved American. Beloved because I not only know France is hosting the 1998 World Cup but, in fact, I am here to see it. A week ago, I was in Tolouse for Cameroon versus Austria. Tomorrow, here in Saint-Etienne, it's Mexico versus Netherlands.

I talk soccer with my new Scottish friends for another stop or two, until we reach the square where nearly everyone exits the tram. It's just a public green in Saint-Etienne's city center, benches and steps, flowers and trees sprouting from squares cut into the concrete. For the tournament, though, a giant television screen has been erected atop a temporary stage, flanked by stacks of speakers and decorated with Cup du Mundial banners.

Outside the tram, it is a bouquet of soccer jerseys—Brazilian yellow, Italian blue, Korean red, and a lot of Dutch orange and Mexican green. I continue on for another stop where the tourism office will fail to find any accommodations left in town and instead offer me the next best thing, an index card with directions to the home of a family who will rent me a room for the night.

Another tram ride, and two busses later, I am so far into the countryside the city and the stadium are lost to hills and towering hedgerows. Though I do not speak French, handing the index card to each bus driver has gotten me to a gravel lane with a two-story, modern-looking stucco house at the end of it. Exactly what was described to me at the tourism office. Before I reach the front steps, the teenage daughter of the family is standing in the doorway, asking if I speak French or Russian as she beckons me inside. It shames me to say just English, to be so typically American, but she is undeterred. She leads me into the kitchen and gives me an ice cream sandwich. I do not want an ice cream sandwich but thank her with one of my five French words, *merci*, and eat it with *mmmmms* and belly pats even though it isn't one of the better ice cream sandwiches I've ever had. She then leads me to my room where she points to where I should drop my backpack and, with excited motions and words I do not understand, has me follow her back downstairs

We step into a quiet living room where three Mexican men are sitting on a couch. They stand for introductions, the one closest to me holding out his hand, "Tomas."

"Robert," I say.

Tomas is about my age, late twenties, early thirties at the most, his hair jet black, short and slightly gelled. The look on his face is some combination of bemusement and surprise without alarm, as though some strange woman has recently given him an ice cream sandwich.

The other two men, Jorge and Eduardo, look like they could be Tomas's uncles—gray hair just starting to appear in their unkempt curls, their eyes a bit puffy, the lines on their cheeks semipermanent after polite grins, though it makes them look experienced more so than old.

Tomas says, "*Habla Espanol*?"

"*Una poquito,*' I say.

"*Un poquito*," he corrects. "Why you," he says and pauses, thinking. He points at the floor. "Why you, Saint-Etienne?"

"*Fútbol*."

Tomas smiles. Jorge nods in approval. Eduardo watches.

The daughter holds out her arms in a gesture of welcome to all. She looks genuinely pleased that we have all said our names and shook hands, that we have started conversing as though we are old friends from the same neighborhood. Or same hemisphere, at least.

Hours later I have settled into the couch with my journal, unwilling to figure out how to reverse the bus directions and get back to town because later, in the dark, after a few drinks, I know I won't be able to find my way back here.

The three Mexican men come into the living room, talking. From their gestures and the occasional cognate, it seems they want to go back to town but aren't sure where to go.

"The square," I interrupt and get blank stares for my effort. "A big T.V.," I add with complementary hand gestures. "Muy people," I say, then wonder if that means "many" or "much." Tomas and Jorge are listening intently, trying to understand. I search my ninth grade Spanish class vocabulary, tip an imaginary beer to my lips, and say, "*Fútbol Fiesta*."

"*Sí*," Tomas says, a kind smile for me.

Jorge, who is tall and skinny and looks awfully serious, says, "Tequila?" I shrug. "Probably."

He jingles the car keys in his pocket, alerting Tomas and Eduardo to follow. At the front door, Jorge stops and looks back, eyebrows raised. "Roberto?" he says, and it's immediately clear: I am to join them, required to find a square I've seen once from a tram in a foreign city.

* * *

A week ago, I turned thirty in Firenze. I went for a long bike ride into the hills outside the city, looped past Roman ruins, and rode hard on the way back. I returned with just enough time to get a sandwich, an expensive bottle of Coca-Cola, and a seat in Piazza Santa Croce where, with a mass of people, I watched a World Cup match on a giant T.V. in the open air.

I'm not totally relaxed being alone in unfamiliar places where I do not speak the language, but I've been pulling this off so far. Any time I feel lost, I put a scowl on my face and glare at street signs and city maps. I talk to myself, loudly, because a five foot eight, one hundred and forty pound guy is only intimidating and not worth mugging if he seems like he could snap at any second. And besides, I'm thirty now. Even before leaving Firenze, I knew I could make it to Saint-Etienne, find a place to stay, and find a ticket for the match.

Sitting in the back of a rented, Euro micro-subcompact, centimeters away from the silent Eduardo, I feel strangely at home. The sound of Tomas and Jorge speaking in the front seat is the Spanish I know from growing up in Southern California, not that formal Madrid stuff or perplexing Catalonian. So when Tomas turns around and asks who I will be rooting for tomorrow, I answer honestly: "Mexico."

"Mexico?" he says, the surprise in his voice just as honest.

"*Sí*," I say but have no way to explain what I am feeling. It's a Southwest thing, I guess. A Spanish accent sounds more melodic than an East Coast or a Southern accent. City names that end in ville or burgh are more foreign than those that begin with *Los* or *San*. I put a finger to my chest, then wave it in a circle to include the four of us. "Norte Americanos."

Tomas nods as though he understands, or at least accepts this.

The "*fútbol fiesta*" is easy to find. Signs lead us to the city center and the square is glowing from blocks away. It is even more crowded than it was in the daytime, orange and green jerseys now dominating the space. Dutch fans are smiles and songs and hugs for anyone wearing orange. Mexican fans are drinks held high from outdoor cafes and *aye-yai-yai's*.

We squeeze into a small bar overflowing with fans. I get a beer. Everyone else gets a margarita on the rocks. One. They make faces, comments I do not understand, and just as Tomas and I are getting into our Spanish 101 conversation—"En Mexico, donde es su casa?" "My house in Mexico City."—Jorge and Eduardo set down their empty glasses. "Tomas," Jorge says, flicking a finger at his drink, which Tomas lifts and finishes dutifully. I set down a half-full beer and follow everyone out the door.

In the crush of people on the square, I fall behind Tomas. He disappears between backs and jerseys, arms and legs. For a minute, I walk blindly forward, scanning left and right for my amigos. "Roberto," I hear without seeing who has said it or if it's even for me. "Roberto,' I hear again and follow the sound up, above the crowd where Jorge's curly head and grim face is maybe ten feet from me. He waves his hand, reeling me in until I break through a wall of people and see Eduardo standing next to Jorge, Tomas just in front welcoming me back with a nod.

At a second bar, everyone again orders a margarita on the rocks while I get a beer. Tomas is curious. "You no like Margarita?"

I tap my head, knowing my words probably won't carry enough meaning. "Tequila doesn't like me."

In truth, tequila and I have a longstanding relationship. When you turn eighteen in Southern California you're too young to step into a bar but you're old enough to leave the country on your own. You don't need a passport. You don't even need to know where to go. The taxi drivers waiting on the other side of the fence know why you're here and they take you directly to Avenida Revolucion, the heart of Tijuana's bar scene. Once you arrive, it's even easier. A "margarita" is a margarita. "Tequila" is tequila. And if you order a "cerveza," the bartender will ask, in English, "Which kind of beer do you want, man?" You pay for everything in American dollars because everything is priced in American dollars.

Other than the Federales walking around outside with their giant guns, it feels pretty American until a waiter starts blowing his whistle in loud, short bursts, letting everyone in the bar know a Tequila Popper is coming. It was always harrowing to me, the way a waiter would circle around a few tables like a shark, making it unclear who was about to go down. And as often as it happened to me, I never got used to having a waiter wrap his towel-draped arm under my chin, tip me back in my chair, pour tequila directly from the bottle into my mouth with that whistle blaring in increasingly shorter and louder bursts. I looked forward to being tipped forward again, to the towel going over my head so the waiter could thrash me back and forth until, finally, he popped me, gently but firmly, on the back of the head and either he or a friend lifted a beer to my lips for a chaser to bring it all to an end.

The Tequila Popper is a rite of passage, like getting beat up to officially join a gang. You feel both humbled your friends would shell out the five bucks when beers are only two-fifty, and totally violated.

This is why, despite Jorge seeing my second beer and saying, "Roberto. Margarita?" I decline. "Cerveza," I say and rub my stomach. "Mmmmmm."

The more I talk to Tomas, the more connected I feel to him. Maybe he looks more Mexican-American to me than Mexican. Like someone who may have gone to my high school. Maybe his eyes are sharper, more Spanish than indigenous. But this makes no sense, because the Mexican-American guys I know in California look both ways too. Maybe it's just that he's really trying hard to converse with me and make me feel included.

Our conversation is slow, but we're making progress. I now understand that Tomas has a career job in communicado. This could mean he's

104

anything from a people-person journalist to an angry I.T. guy, but it's enough for now. He knows I am a student, though I don't bother to say I've just finished my MA and am moving on to an MFA. I have no idea how to explain, in Spanish, an MFA in Creative Writing. I can barely explain it in English to my father.

We leave the second bar after one drink, Jorge and Eduardo having again made faces at their margaritas. The third stop is an outdoor café on the square. Jorge finds us a table right on the street side, right on the railing. We see everybody who walks by and whenever they're wearing Mexico green, someone starts chanting, "Meh-he-co, Meh-he-co," and we all join in.

If I am understanding Tomas correctly, he has a home, a wife, and a baby daughter back in Mexico. Since starting graduate school, these are the things that visit me on occasion just before I fall asleep: *You're almost thirty and you're still in school. You don't have a career, a home, a child, a wife, or even a dog. What are you doing with your life?*

In the morning, most days, the rays of truth keep me happy: I'm doing something brave. I left a career job in advertising to pursue a career as a writer. I teach college classes and neither of my parents has a bachelor's degree. I've been dating undergraduates for the past year and a half—something I almost never did when I was an undergraduate. And midway through my final semester, I began dating a fellow grad student who sees eye-to-eye with me on politics, religion, and football. And she's gorgeous. In Rome, just a couple days before turning thirty, I wrote in my journal that I was happy with the choices I'd made, with what the future held, and that my only regret so far was that I still didn't own a dog.

But here's Tomas, roughly the same age as me, having just as much fun. Only, in a few weeks he'll return to the bosom of North America—home, family, job. Maybe even a dog. I'll return to a summer job freelancing at an advertising agency in California, then leave for a cheap, roach-friendly apartment near the University of Alabama campus in time for fall classes. I want to pick Tomas's brain: are you as happy as you seem? Is the nuclear family as good as it sounds?

Instead, we struggle through our barely bilingual conversation. Some guys in Mexico jerseys are hanging over the railing, talking to Jorge and Eduardo. One of them is wearing a backpack, and when Jorge apparently lets him in on the tequila situation—that you cannot make a decent margarita when you start with bad tequila—this man pulls from his backpack a two liter sized bottle of authentic, Mexican tequila. He holds it aloft like the World Cup and Jorge and Eduardo cheer. Tomas and I join in and our newest amigo hops over the railing and pops the top off the bottle, ready to share the bounty of old Mexico.

After topping off everyone's margarita like a waiter, he steps behind Jorge and everyone knows what's next. Jorge leans his head back and a smooth stream of golden liquid pours and pours, a lot longer than anything I'd ever seen in Tijuana. Jorge's head comes forward, a smile and a thumbs-up to Eduardo; this is the real stuff.

After Eduardo has a go, the man with the bottle skips past me and stands behind Tomas who dutifully leans his head back and takes his shot.

Jorge then points to me, "Roberto."

The man with the bottle does not question this and in a moment is standing at my shoulder. "No thanks," I say to him.

Jorge's face is grim again. "Roberto? Tequila!" he says, as if this explains everything.

"*Gracias*, no" I say to him.

"*Sí*, Roberto," Jorge says, his face loosening a little, a good uncle. "*Sí*," Eduardo says.

"Roberto," somebody from the other side of the railing says. "*Sí*."

Tomas is a warm smile and brotherly reassurance, "*Sí*, Roberto."

I'm thirty years old, so why does it feel like I'm eighteen and in Tijuana, the drink already paid for, my friends watching, and the question not if I'll do it but how well it will go.

"*Sí*," I say, leaning my head back and closing my eyes.

The tequila is syrup at the back of my throat. My draw is smooth, longer than any popper at eighteen, nineteen, or twenty years-old. The pourer actually stops before I wave him off.

Leaning forward, eyes opening, Eduardo is there, my beer in his hand. He offers it to me the way a mother extends a cool rag for your feverish forehead. But my taste buds search and discover no reason to wince or gag. "No," I shake off the beer. "I got it."

"No?" Eduardo says.

I give him a short, slow, affirming shake, as much for myself as him. "No."

Eduardo clangs the beer onto the metal table and his arm is up, over, and around me. "Now," he says, pulling me in closer, tighter, "you are a Mexican."

My amigos, the man with the bottle, the people on the other side of the railing, cheer. Jorge toasts me with his awful Margarita, "Roberto!"

Tomas smiles and holds up his Margarita in tribute.

We linger at this café a while longer, our conversations growing faster on the back of alcohol and some perceived, assumed, understanding. We are men. We are football fans. We are Mexicans.

We end the night with bar Tequila and orange juice. It tastes so refreshing until we're back in the car. Minutes into the ride, I have to hold on tight so the subcompact will stop lifting off the highway and tumbling around. When Eduardo notices, he clasps hands with me like an army buddy, like a surgeon is sawing off my leg and we both want me to make it. I focus on the fact that a man my age has no business barfing after a night of drinking. That, and I'm certain Eduardo will revoke my Mexican status if I throw up even bad, French tequila.

* * *

My headache and dry mouth wake me. In the dining room, Jorge, Eduardo, and Tomas are dressed, blue jeans and green jerseys, the remnants of eggs and pastries laid out before them.

"Coffee?" Tomas says gently because, clearly, he is seeing what I am feeling.

Jorge motions me to sit. He pours me a cup of French press coffee and hands it down the table through Eduardo's hands.

Tomas explains in gestures and cognates that they are leaving soon but will wait for me. I can't imagine moving fast enough to get dressed, packed, and out the door without my head tumbling off my shoulders and smashing to the floor. I turn down their generous gift of time, a ride, and companionship.

We say our goodbyes in the front hall, a handshake and firm nod from Jorge, a genuine smile from Eduardo. Another warm smile and a last wave from Tomas.

At game time, the sky is a warm, gray blanket that delivers rain in patches. By the time I arrive outside the stadium, the men selling tickets from their pockets are asking too many Francs for a match that started ten minutes ago. My head is functional but unhappy. My stomach, however, is ready for some food. I decide to forgo the match in lieu of a meal and a crowd-beating early train to Paris. On board, I'll check the schedule of matches and then either head to another city or keep going to Belgium which, suddenly, seems so quaint, calm and appealing.

The Saint-Etienne train station is set up for a massive evacuation, temporary barricades in place to funnel people into and through the lobby to the platforms. At the moment, however, it's like being in Disneyland before the park opens. The pavement is free of even a slip of paper or a piece of gum. I stroll through the lines to find my train empty and delayed, like all the other northbound trains, until after the match is over.

From my seat in the dining car, I hear the crowds coming just before the platform is awash in orange and green. Unwittingly, I've chosen the green train. Or at least, the green car. Mexican fans, dancing and chanting, smiling and hugging, flood the dining car.

At first, no one asks to join me at my table. They fill the other seats, cram three people into two spots, stand and hold the rails. Finally, a young guy asks, in English, if he can sit.

Though he is Mexican and wearing a green jersey, David is from Torrance, California. Translated: about thirty minutes from where I grew up. When I ask for details about the match, his accent is perfect Southern California: "Oh, dude, it was an awesome game." First, he gives me the highlights of Mexico's comeback from two goals down to earn a tie and secure a place in the next stage of the tournament. He then gives me his other highlight: he's got tickets to a different match but will now try to sell them and use the money for Mexico's next match; he's a first-generation son of immigrants and about to graduate from Cal State Dominguez Hills with a journalism degree and is waffling about graduate school; and since I went to graduate school, can I tell him if it's worth it?

I can't tell him what to do, but my answers polish grad school up nicely in the hazy, late afternoon light and he tells me it sounds like a great experience.

Tequila shots start making their rounds and David goes in search of a bottle. Rather than give in or say no, I lean back in my seat, close my eyes and feign sleep. The summer sun sets late in northern Europe and I'm traveling norte on a fiesta train. For the moment, I am feeling very American, not at all Mexican, but very much at home.

Tequila Sunrise
Julie Chappell

He walks in beauty like the night
as another shot and a beer
size him up in the
smoke-filled neon of the place
where in the closing hours
you check for latex shield
to guard your virgin heart
and shield him from
the dry, cold within.

Yet another shot and his eyes
turn that blue-green that once
sent you lustful and squirming
for the ride.

One more, another and his
sharp-edged look grows soft and
fills your lust with longing
for the one you left behind.

One last shot and he's the ride of your life—

for a few hours
until his blood-trimmed eyes
lose that blue-green cast
and the sharp-edge returns
with ketone-bodied breath
in a dawn
empty

Norma Brown, "Lemon and Lime"

A Little Rain in Arkansas
George Wallace

professor fear and his longhair piano
sat on the bandstand
he was just about to play
some boogie-woogie
when somebody fresh
from pontchartrain
with a three-piece suit
walked in—did you
see that thing go down,
bartender? he walked
right into a baobob tree
he walked right into
a needle of smoke
he walked right into
a girl with a margarita
she was addicted to jazz
he was a blues pantomime
he smoked like sweet tokay
she was a bottle of news
they stepped on up to
the front of the line
it was a low-key thing
there was nobody else
there was no good reason
there was a little rain in arkansas
there was an overnight train
to new orleans—they
took that train

Tequila Brings Peace to Mideast
Jeffrey DeLotto

I'm holding his prayer beads in my hand right now, the sunlight catching the flush-set silver screws in each black-lacquered bead, the silk tassel draped down from my palm, and I'd like to tell you his name was Abdullah, but to tell the truth I don't remember (you know how tequila is).

I was teaching English at Yarmouk University in Irbid, Jordan, a provincial city about fifteen miles south of the Syrian border—1981 it was, and the Iraq-Iran War was on, Jordan siding with Iraq, Syria with Iran, but we didn't pay much attention to that, except when the tank and artillery transport trucks jammed up the roads.

Why Jordan? After three years teaching at Tech in Lubbock, Texas, and me from Florida, I wanted far away. Turned out that Irbid has a climate remarkably close to Lubbock, but I hadn't known that then, and the water was better....

Well, Ben was throwing a Christmas party next door. He taught ESL, was gay, was classified black in the States, and was always questioned by the Arab border guards because they saw Benjamin as a Jewish name, but he was a social butterfly and played a hell of a piano, so his parties were always a big draw. He shared the flat with a stocky Danish computer programmer named Torkill (that's what it sounded like anyway), who had a Peugeot that could drive up the wall of a wadi, so I had excellent neighbors.

The sweep and roll of a Gershwin tune tumbled out of the flat as I stepped across the way, hardly feeling the bite of cold wind before pushing through a crowd of coats and cigarette smoke in the entryway to the kitchen, setting a bottle of Cuervo Silver toward the back of the counter, turning to greet Nick and Sue Ashby, two Brits recently from teaching posts at a university in Mosul, Iraq. They were of course building tepid gin and tonics.

Time wore on, I squeezed past Ben's entourage near the fuel-oil furnace, found no available ambulatory females, and wandered back to the kitchen to recharge, lighting one of those delicious unfiltered camels I smoked before I wanted to live a long time and poured another shot of tequila, picked up a quarter lemon (limes were impossible to find) from my bowl, salted my hand, bit, knocked back, and licked. I was feeling Christmassy already.

This young Arab fellow, dressed very sharp, was watching this new-to-him drinking ritual with fascination, stopped working the prayer beads with his right hand, and stepped over, wanted to know what I was doing....

"Shootin' tequila—wanna learn?"

I suspected—hell, I knew—he was Muslim, but if I had a dollar for every Baptist or Muslim I saw down a drink, my 401K would be in a lot better shape.

Abdullah wasn't exactly a slow learner, but we both wanted to make sure he got the rhythm right, and that took some modeling, too—and of course we solved many problems and became very good friends before the bottle was done, such good friends that he insisted I keep his beads as his symbol of our shared moments.

I have them still.

El Patrón
Karla K. Morton

I woke up smiling, riffs of *Super Freak*
pinballing in my brain; makeup caked, black
mascara smeared, teeth like wet dryer lint;
a yard-sale of clothes tossed around the bed

in my naked nose-dive into the sheets;
hips, feet, deliciously sore... *Ah*, but I
owned the dance floor last night. I shimmied, twirled
and wantonly grinded in a great mash

of glowing humanity, the bass, drums,
a collective heartbeat. I didn't like
tequila until I was 44;
mother's words warning against the evil—

in case all those family rumours *were* true,
in case there was Indian blood in us.
It'd make you crazy, she said, *make you sleep*
with men you wouldn't normally sleep with...

Straight-walking, I swore I didn't like it,
until I tried the good stuff—*El Patrón*;
learned to salt and lick the back of my hand;
down it in one gulp; bite into the lime;

then slam that sticky shot-glass upside down...
my new secret secret to happiness—
letting the soul step out, unchaperoned
to jive and groove and flirt with the body;

to let blue agave sing through my blood
like cool ancient rivers... I reach over
to the other side of the bed, *hoping*
that mound of sleeping man is my husband.

Agave Puzzle
Ebbesen Davis

Stereo (3D) photography involves making paired images from slightly different angles. When our eyes are presented with the appropriate left and right images, we see a 3D effect. The real magic takes place in the brain, which interpolates data from two images to create a space with lifelike depth and dimension. To experience the 3D effect of this image pair, fix your gaze on a center-point between the two images. Next, shift your focus beyond these photos, allowing your eyes to relax until a third image appears in the middle. Then, shift your attention to the middle image until you see a single 3D image. This unique visual puzzle is provided for those who enjoy unusual challenges. However, in our experience, tequila consumed beyond moderation reverses the effect described above. Special thanks to Bob Gillett of 24 Diner in Austin, Texas for the fine Chinaco Añejo pictured here.

Christmas Proof

song lyric by A. William Hinson

Santa—don't stop here tonight
with more junk that I can't use.
Marie just left and took the kids,
and I've got the Christmas blues.
Salt and limes and shots of José Cuervo
are lined up for inspection.
They go down the counter and around the sink—
my entire shot glass collection.

Don't want to hear your cheerful ho-ho-ho
or reindeer on my roof.
Anything that comes down my chimney—
better be Smith & Wesson proof.

Drink a shot with salt and lime
then toss the empty in the air.
Shoot it down and grab another round
until I fall from this chair.

Don't want to hear your cheerful ho-ho-ho
or reindeer on my roof.
I'm gonna shoot these shooters down tonight
until I'm Christmas Proof.

It's a party I'm confessin'
with José Cuervo and Smith & Wesson,
we're shootin' holes through the roof,
and we'll party here until I'm Christmas Proof.

The Tab
Lyman Grant

Lee and Judy and I are riffing off each other
Assigning various colleagues to one of Dante's
Circles in Hell. *We know where I belong*, I say,
Let the winds swirl and the seas heave, I'll hang
With Helen, Cleopatra, and Francesca. Here's to love
And lust. May we never know the difference. I grab
The wedge of lime, salt my hand, raise my shot of Hornitos,
And touch their glasses lightly like a kiss on chaste
Cheeks. Lee and Judy sip their Mexican Martinis.
Judy lets her lips drift down the rim as if in afterthought.
We are huddled around our usual table on the usual
Third Thursday at Matt's El Rancho. Between us are
Spinach quesadillas and a bizarre cheese concoction
That Judy always orders. It could clog the heart
Just sitting there congealing in its cooling bowl.
Lee jabs it with a chip and stirs it clockwise. A graceful
Twist and lift of the fist shocks with its beauty.
I'm being good and refrain. During one of our first
Dates, my astonished first wife commented that she
Had never known anyone, before me, who drank
Tequila in tumblers. I smacked her hard on the mouth
Then tossed her the keys to the Volkswagon bus.
Three times we stopped that night on the way home
Before I could free myself of my enthusiasms.
Judy and Lee start up on the "psychopath from work,"
Their phrase. We talk about her every time we meet.
They've got her down there in the ninth ring. This will
Go a long time, so we order another round, mine
A double and a Corona as chaser. My sisters
Once persuaded me to steal two glasses from the Cadillac
Bar in Nuevo Laredo. They were drinking age. I was
Sixteen and had a Sprite or something. It was the first
Vacation since our mother had died. We'd been
To the bull fights like we used to do, and my dad wanted
A tequila sour like he used to drink with Mom

When she made these trips. "Wait till no one's
Looking, then slip them in the bag with the *huaraches*,"
My sisters repeated. When I turned them over in the motel,
The rims were sticky and crusted with salt. Looking back...
No, it does no good to look back. There's a picture of Sharon
And me and Will as a baby at Chuy's. We use to go there
Friday nights after swimming laps at Deep Eddy Pool.
It's an incredibly cleaned out feeling swimming a mile
In that cool water. So many swimmers you'd have to do
Circles. Then the taco plate and a couple of margaritas.
After a work party, eight years later, I almost left Chuy's
With a married professor in the department. It's a mistake
I'm glad I didn't make. Wonder what ring she's confined to?
What goes around comes around, Judy is saying, still talking
About the psychopath. I bring up her daughter. She's tying
The knot to a nice guy from an old Austin family.
What's it cost, I ask about the diamond. Judy rolls
Her eyes. She wants to tell me, but I shouldn't have asked.
Then I remember to tell them about the tequila tasting
I attended at the UT Club last week. Will went with me.
Pure Agaves. Some with notes of vanilla. Another hinted
Of ginger, I swear. All paired with hors d'oeuvres. Some
Cost a hundred bucks a bottle. Will preferred the clear ones,
Snuck seconds on a couple of them. Lee asked me my favorite.
Can't remember, I say. *I am blessed with indiscriminate
Tastes*. The waiter wonders by to check on us, picks up
Some plates and empties. Makes eye contact. Another round?

Lisa Craig, "Coronarita" at Las Casas in Temple, Texas

A Day in the Life of an Insurance Adjuster
Jim Spurr

About a mile or so on north of there
you'll see a white pickup
in the driveway. Might be
sorta gray and white.
On the west side. I think.
Anyway if the renter is home
you won't miss her. She'll
be in the front yard
tanning or something.
She's a looker. Believe me.
You'll know you're at
the right place. If you see her.

He was right.
She was in the yard dancing
alone. Barefoot. Eyes closed.
Knees together. Arms straight up.
A thin cigarette in one hand.
Margarita in the other.
Listening to Country & Western. W
e were told she had been dating
a C&W star. Don't know which
one. She wasn't much of a talker.

But as bad as those directions were
this was no doubt the right house.
Sat in my car a while just watching.
Wishing
I had brought some José Cuervo
Margarita mix.
A guitar... and could sing just a little.

all my doors are open
Steven Schroeder

the wind blows where it will, and you hear the sound, but you
do not know... (John 3:8)

Pull my daisy / Tip my cup / Cut my thoughts / for coconuts
(Allen Ginsberg, Jack Kerouac, and Neal Cassady)

1

begin with the glass all empty

run a wedge of lime
around the rim

stand it on its head
in coarse salt

chill.

count one
cointreau and one
lime juice, two

tequila, silver. mix.
pour over ice.

empty

2

again, begin again.

3

all may be omitted save
spirit, which must be present

in a ratio of three or more to one

if you expect (and you should

always expect) a great wind
and tongues of fire

scattered over every circle of friends

4

remember wind
blows where it will
and you hear it, though

you know nothing

5

consider how a daisy works:

it does not labor, it does not spin,

yet even, you know, Solomon

6

all my doors are open

7

empty, begin again.

The Number You Have Reached
Melvin Sterne

You walk into a diner at nine o'clock Sunday morning smoking a fat Torpedo Figurado and carrying a $350 bottle of Sol Añejo. The diner is empty. There is a long, white counter stretched out to your right. A half-dozen, crappy, orange-upholstered booths line the wall to your left, with as many tables in between, but not a customer in the place. The floor is grimy. Most of the tables are piled with dirty dishes. You pick the cleanest spot you can find on the counter, right next to the cash register, and sit down on one of those roundy-round stools with the chrome-plated footrests. You prop your elbows on the Formica. It is cool and slightly greasy. You take a swig from the bottle and almost finish it. It's your second bottle since you swiped a Conde Nast fake-leather backpack off the back seat of an open Corvette convertible last night. You didn't know there were tequila and cigars in the backpack, you just got lucky. You kept the tequila but you ditched the backpack right away. The booze doesn't even burn anymore. You set the bottle down on the counter with a satisfying twack. There is a radio playing faintly from the back room. You pick out the strains of Kenny Loggins and Dolly Parton crooning "Islands in the Stream."

The grill is on. There are two pots half-filled with black, rendered-down coffee on electric burners directly in front of you. There are cooked link sausages piled on a towel by the grill and crisp, dry bacon stacked on a plate beside them. You smell the meat and your mouth waters. You haven't eaten in more than a day. "Hello?" you say. You take a puff off the cigar and exhale in the direction of the grill. Kenny and Dolly ask, "How can we be wrong?" Offhand, you can think of about five hundred ways. You get up and walk around the counter and peer into the back room.

The cook is sitting on a five gallon plastic bucket with his feet up on another bucket and his back against the wall by the walk-in cooler. The door to the cooler is open. He is smoking a cigarette. He has a Lone Star long-neck clenched between his knees, and a half-dozen empties scattered at his feet. The air above him is hazy. There is a mountain of butts on the floor. Under his apron he wears a sweat-stained tee shirt and some grubby jeans.

You drum your fingers on the door and clear your throat. "Good morning," you say.

"Screw you," he replies.

"Rough day?" you ask.

"Let me tell you about a rough day," he says, rising. You wish you hadn't asked.

He chugs his beer and brushes past you into the front room. He takes a swig of your tequila—empties it—then flings the bottle through the plate glass window just above and slightly to the right of the faded red letters that say Julia's Home Cooking. The letters have green and gold outlines, and some holly and berries trim left over from Christmas. Or maybe it was lettuce and tomatoes. The paint is faded and the artwork iffy. The bottle punches through the window and the glass cascades onto the sidewalk outside and startles a cat that was stalking a pigeon. The cat goes one way and the pigeon the other. You think they have the right idea.

The cook turns and makes like he's going to stab his finger into the middle of your forehead. You ask, "Can I have a cup of coffee and a menu?" The cook stops, his arm coiled in mid-strike. He unties his apron and tosses it on the grill, walks into the cooler and comes out lugging a case of Lone Star on his shoulder.

"Screw you," he says again as he passes, "and your coffee." As an afterthought he pauses and scoops a handful of bills from the till and stuffs them in his pocket. After he leaves, the apron begins to smoke.

It is July and already 95 degrees outside. The clock on the wall says nine oh five. There is no traffic on the street. The tequila is fading and you feel a world-class hangover coming on. Six months ago you left your wife and daughter in Burlington, Vermont. You'd been drinking for forty-eight hours and your wife had been complaining about it for forty-seven. You told her you were going to the store for a bottle of milk and a paper. Instead you bought another bottle of Curevo and drove to New Jersey, where you stopped under a freeway and sold the tires off your car for $100. You bought another bottle from Tiki's Liquors, because it was close, and a Greyhound ticket to Atlanta because your car wasn't going anywhere without tires.

"Hello," you say, but there is no sound except the drone of the compressor in the cooler. You come around the counter to the grill and pick up the apron, which is smoking but not yet burst into flames. You wipe down the grill with it and throw it away. Dolly and Kenny have stopped singing. You are listening to 88.6 Country Proud. Soybeans are down a nickel. The National Weather Service is forecasting another drought. Corn weevils have reached epidemic proportions.

You pour yourself a cup of coffee and it is bitter, so you pour half of it out and fill it back up with milk and sugar. It is bad but you drink it anyway. When you get to the bottom of the cup the sugar washes the burnt taste away. You open the little fridge under the counter and find a pitcher of OJ next to a carton of eggs and a white plastic tub full of grated potatoes.

There is a mountain of hash browns on the grill and a half-dozen eggs sizzling sunny side up when the first customer walks through the door. He sits down where you were sitting and looks around. Just for kicks you plop a menu in front of him, give the counter a half-hearted swipe with a wet rag, and pour him a glass of water. "What'll you have?" you ask.

"Waffles" he says.

"Can't," you reply.

"Iron's broke."

"Pancakes then."

You don't remember seeing batter in the cooler but you look anyway. "Out of batter," you say.

"What have you got?"

"Eggs."

You serve him eggs and hash browns, throw in a side order of sausage for free. You pour him a cup of coffee but he complains about it. You take his cup, taste it, then pour half of it out and fill it back up with leftover milk from a glass on the counter. Then, while he watches, you fill the cup with sugar until it overflows.

"That's disgusting," he says.

On his way out the door you say: "Ya'll come back now, ya here?" You go to the cooler and open a beer. You eat the eggs and sausage.

After a while a very old woman in a blue granny dress and black, square-toed shoes comes in. She is wearing a plastic, imitation straw hat covered with small, pink plastic flowers. She walks with a stainless steel cane. She shuffles to the booth in the furthest corner and sits down, raps the table with her cane, says: "Julius, I'm home." She stares into space. You ignore her.

A minute later two men come in. One is tall and thin, dressed in a black suit with a white shirt and string cowboy tie. He wears a ridiculously small black cowboy hat with a silver Navajo band around it. He reminds you of a mortician you knew when you were a child.

The other man is in a wheelchair. He wears a genuine Panama hat and a green Hawaiian shirt with blue parrots printed on it. He has a plaid

125

blanket over his knees. He wears dark glasses. He is older, sixty maybe. His face is bony, skeletal.

A kid comes to the door on a skateboard, leans in, says, "Nasty," then boards away. His hair is orange. You hate the sound of skates on pavement.

You finish your beer and look around for your cigar. You find it. It is still lit. The old woman raps the table with her cane. The men look around at the mess. After a while you pick up an order pad and saunter over to their table. "Hiya, creeky," you say to the man in the wheelchair. "What'll ya have?"

"This table's dirty," he says.

"No shit?" you reply.

You go behind the counter and find a gray plastic bus tub. You pick it up and get a wad of old, warm butter on your hand. You put it down and wipe the butter on a rag. You can still feel it under your nails. You return to the table and pile the dishes, glasses, cups, and silverware in the tub and wipe the table down. You empty the tub into the garbage. The glasses break. The old lady raps her cane on the table. The kid skates by on his board again. You notice that his orange hair is worked up into shiny spikes. He is wearing a bright, steel chain around his hips. You presume he wants to look tough. You wonder how long it takes him to make up his hair. The men order bacon and eggs.

Somewhere in Appalachia you left the Greyhound with an albino girl named Carol to spend the weekend in a cabin by a lake. She promised that it was beautiful and said it once belonged to her father, but he had sold it to a U.S. Senator from Idaho who lived in D.C. and used it for a love nest. She said he used to bring his interns there to make home porno movies. She didn't tell you how she knew this. She had pink eyes. Even her pubic hair was white.

The cabin had one room, no electricity, no furniture. There was nothing to eat except some beef jerky you found, evidently forgotten at the back of the top shelf of the cabinet. You did it dogstyle on the floor. You got splinters in your knees. The roof was covered with dead leaves and green mold. The outside boards weathered gray. It leaned to the south.

The lake was pond-sized and scummy. Cattails overran the shallows and lily pads smothered everything else. You paddled around naked in the afternoon in a tipsy rowboat. It was her idea. You tried to make love but the mosquitoes ate you alive. The boat seeped amber water. It smelled froggy. When you ran out of tequila you walked to town to buy more. You stopped in the bar for a cool one. You forgot your way back. After a while you gave up looking and bought a bus ticket to Knoxville. You were disappointed not to have found any movies of the senator.

Willie Nelson sings "Blue Eyes Cryin' in the Rain" on the radio. You scramble the eggs with the shells and burn the toast. You serve it to the two men, but they don't seem to notice. "We need to talk," they say. They gesture towards an empty chair.

"Would you like a beer?" you ask. They nod.

While you're in the cooler you think about the possibilities.

"Things aren't working out," says the man who looks like an undertaker.

"I guess not," you reply.

"We're going to have to take a new direction."

"I'm not very good at directions," you say. They look at each other.

"Do you understand what we're saying?" First you nod. Then you shake your head.

You were sleeping in the doorway of a pawnshop near the civic center in downtown Knoxville at two o'clock in the morning when a policeman tapped you on the foot with his nightstick and asked what you were doing.

You told him you wanted to be first in line to buy Elvis memorabilia in the morning. He told you to move along.

You told him to screw himself.

He and his partner threw you in the river. Then they arrested you for swimming after dark.

It is illegal to swim in the Tennessee River within the city limits of Knoxville after dark. The fine was $50. Someone called your wife and she paid it. Evidently there was a "Missing Person Report" on you. The cops asked what's what and you told them you're not missing a thing. Your wife cried on the phone. She said your daughter missed you. She wanted you to go to treatment. She said her father would foot the bill. You know he hates you. You think he might bribe the nurses to put meds in your food and keep you forever. You think about Jack Nicholson in *One Flew Over the Cuckoo's Nest*. The cops took you to the Salvation Army Mission while your wife went to wire you a plane ticket home.

That afternoon you hit the jackpot panhandling and bought a bottle of La Pinata. You hitched a ride to Tulsa with a meth-addicted trucker named Phil. He stopped in Little Rock and wanted you to suck his dick. He pulled his pants down around his ankles and tried to get hard and put on a condom. You ran away with his wallet. He looked funny chasing you down the highway and pulling up his pants at the same time. You think it served him right.

"Perhaps we're not being clear," says the man in the wheelchair. "Let me try a different approach. May I call you Larry?"

You shrug. "Sure."

The men look puzzled. "Your name is Larry, isn't it?" asks the undertaker.

"That depends on who's asking," you say. "Are you with the IRS?" They shake their heads.

"Then I might be Larry. I could be Larry."

The man in the wheelchair pulls a pistol from under the blanket and you lunge for it. The two of you tumble onto the floor. You have almost pried the gun out of his hand when the undertaker crashes a chair across your back. Unlike in the movies, the chair does not break. Your back does not break, either, but it hurts like hell. You flip the pistol away from the wheelchair man with what you think might be your last, dying breath. The undertaker kicks you and you feel something snap in your hip. He straddles your back and pounds your head with his fists. You force yourself onto your hands and knees and find a steak knife on the floor miraculously close to your left hand. You jab the undertaker in the meaty part of his thigh. He rises like a shot. You expect something bad to happen but nothing does. The undertaker hops out the door howling. Creeky rights his wheelchair and hefts into it. One wheel wobbles wildly as he leaves. The old woman beats the table furiously with her cane. In sports, the Mets beat the Cardinals nine to three. Carlos Beltran hit two home runs including a grand slam in the pivotal fifth.

You stagger to the door. Your hip hurts too bad to run. Outside, the boy with the orange hair sprawls on the sidewalk. His skateboard is upside down. The wheels are spinning. Creeky's wheelchair lies on its side. One wheel has fallen off. There is a trail of blood spots leading to an empty parking space. A black Lincoln trailing blue smoke peels around the corner.

You look at the orange headed kid.

"Gnarly," he says. He sits up. He is wearing a dog collar. His face is scratched.

You remember that you are on your way to Seattle. You think it might be a good time to leave but you can't resist the temptation to snag a six-pack of beer. It might come in handy—especially since Larry (you presume he was Larry) finished off your tequila. On your way to the cooler

128

you check the till to see if Larry missed anything. He took all the bills, but you scoop a cool handful of quarters. You check the cooler. Evidently, Larry also hogged all the beer. When you come out of the cooler a policeman blocks the door.

When you left Little Rock, you hitch-hiked north to St. Paul. You thought a change of scene might do you good. In St. Paul you worked two days at a farmers' market. They paid you in cash and vegetables. On the second day you emptied the till and hopped a west-bound freight. You took three bottles of Patron and a bag of limes with you, but you forgot the salt. Still, it was better than nothing. The next night, in Cheyenne, a hobo climbed into your boxcar. He told you his name was Willie and he was a famous bluesman. He said he had a hundred-dollar harmonica but he wouldn't show it to you. He did show you pictures of his family. They were all ugly as sin but you didn't tell him this. "They understand me," he said. His wife had a boyfriend, but he slept on the couch in the winter when Willie came home. You said that was considerate. That's the exact word you used. After you and Willie killed the last bottle, you took turns throwing limes at cows grazing near the tracks.

You told Willie about your daughter, Angelina, and how she loves you unconditionally. She brings you beers from the fridge. You taught her the labels so she could tell one brand from another. You tell her, "Bring me a Tecate," and she brings you a Tecate. Your wife does not approve of this. Willie nodded sympathetically. "Women," he said. While you were sleeping off the tequila, he stole your jacket and what was left of your money. You woke up lonely in Bonners Ferry. That's where you found the Corvette with the Conde Nast fake-leather backpack with the bottles of Sol Añejo and the Figurados. You wished it had more than two bottles, but beggars can't be choosy. Still, you called the owner a "effing cheap bastard."

The policeman asks you for some ID and you tell him about Willie and the train ride from St. Paul. He is not impressed. Not even with the bit about the harmonica. They fingerprint you at the lock-up. You tell them your name is Jefferson Davis and you are a U.S. Senator from Idaho. They bring in the old woman but she doesn't know where she is, much less who you are. They ask if you've ever been arrested before and you think about telling them about swimming after dark in the Tennessee River. You decide not to tell them. The cops are perplexed. Evidently there is no longer a "Missing Person Report" out on you. They check their computer and smoke some cigarettes without offering you one.

Since you didn't take anything tangible, they can't bust you for stealing.

You tell them you panhandled the quarters but nobody cares about them anyway. The café owner doesn't know you from Adam. He says he hired a fry cook named Larry to run the breakfast shift. You claim you were beat up by a man in a wheelchair. Nobody believes you, even though they have the wheelchair. They show you the pistol and ask if you know anything about it. You tell them it is safer standing behind it than in front of it. They charge you with destruction of property. They take your shoelaces and your belt.

You tell them you know your rights and you are entitled to make a phone call. You swagger when you say this. They take you to a pay phone in the hall. You think it is about time to check in with your wife and tell her you are all right. You call collect. You get a recording. The number you have reached is no longer in service.

"That's odd," you say.

You call your father-in-law, in Camden, but he won't take a collect call. You know he is a cheapskate so you call him again on your dime. It actually costs two dollars for the first three minutes. "Robert," you say. "It's me, Sid. You're not going to believe this, but I can't get through to Susan." Robert hangs up and the phone eats your quarters. The guard looks at you. "I see," you say. "That bad? A whole week, huh?" You cover the mouthpiece and say to the guard, "Storms back east, phone lines are down."

Across the hall is a door with a big window of wire-reinforced glass in the middle of it. Inside you see the orange-headed kid talking to a couple of cops. They've emptied the kid's pockets and you see an iPod, some change, and what looks like a tube of glue.

"Well," you say, "I'll try again later. Tell her I'm in jail in Bonner's Ferry and I need her to post bail."

When you hang up the cop says you're in Pocatello, not Bonner's Ferry. You shrug and wonder how you got there. He asks if you want to call anybody else. You can't think of anybody. You have fifty cents in your pocket. A local call is seventy-five.

Love Poem
for Brenda
Robert Wynne

Nothing reminds me more
Of you, than the faint smell of good

Tequila. Remember draining a whole bottle
In that hot tub in cold rain?
Meteors could have landed next to us and
Even still we would've been

Locked in each other's arms.
I'll never taste Black Cherry
Koolaid again without agave
Echoing like it did as we chased

That *Patrón*, swig after swig keeping
Hushed faces flush above steaming water.
Every day is a haystack full of needles.

Please remember how easy this is, like
Rain giving in to gravity.
Early mornings dawn quietly, and we
Snake around
Each other
Nestled in this heap of covers. Sometimes I
Think I must still be dreaming.

Dual Dominance
Joyce Gullickson

Most compromises are the strong, silent type
empty bottles on the table, shoes left by the door
the snifter of brandy, swirled alone
the lyric brogue of Irish whiskey
the false confidence of a few too many.
Those headstrong voices in your mind
insistently urging just one more.
Tequila shots and rime working off each other
as dual dominance is conquered by liquor's lazy eye.
Fish swim into focus,
unwilling to feed the hungry.
How the moon affects the tides
the salt of indifference rimming the glass.
Imagine the boy, a fisherman's son
Where do good men go when they can't go home.
But the barkeeps "No" is non-negotiable—
As keeper of all things holy, and your keys
confess to sacred excess, honor him,
compromise, and call a cab.

Tasty Tequila Teacakes
Barrie Scardino

Teacakes are approximately the same thing as cupcakes, just without any frosting. You may frost these if you wish and call them cupcakes—but then you lose the pleasing alliteration.

Preheat oven to 350°

Get all the following ingredients out to make sure you have everything before you start, or you will hate yourself for having to run to the store in the middle of baking.

2 cups sugar (granulated and refined as a Southern debutante)
4 large eggs (free-range, fair-market, organic chickens recommended for political reasons we are not able to fully explain here)
2 sticks butter (unsalted and softened; you could use salted butter and leave out the salt, but, if your cakes turn out to be awful, it will be your fault)
3 ½ cups flour (bleached all-purpose)
½ tsp salt (Kosher or sea)
1 tbsp baking powder (regular)
¾ cup milk (any %, we use skim to protect our figure—don't laugh, any little sacrifice helps)
¾ cup Tequila (cheap, gold)
1 lime skin (grated)—squeeze the juice from leftover lime insides for margaritas

1. Taste the tequila to make sure it is okay. Maybe twice.

2. In a smallish bowl blend the flour, baking powder, and salt. (The first time I made these, I put the sugar in here too—don't do that. Sugar goes in the next step.)

3. In your biggest bowl, mix (with some electrical tool) the butter, sugar, and lime zest (fancy for grated lime skin).

4. Add eggs, one at a time, beating each one until it is blended in the

butter-sugar mixture (step 2) before adding the next one. Then add a little milk then a little flour, alternating them until they are all used up and it looks like cake batter. (Phew! Finally.)

5. Bake about 25 minutes until golden brown in cupcake tins, preferably with hand-decorated cup-cake liners (see Martha Stewart for decorating ideas). While they are baking, read some poetry and have another tequila.

Makes 19. This recipe should make 24—two 12-muffin-tins' worth—but in our advanced test kitchen, it makes 19 because we overfill the little cupcake liners (about ⅔ full) so there will be delicious muffin tops, so you can eat off of the tops of 3 or 4 cakes before serving to your guests— but remember, then you will only have 15 to actually serve. If you have children, give them the left over cake bottoms. A little tequila won't hurt them, and they won't know the difference anyway. WARNING: You too will have a muffin top if you eat too many of the tasty cakes.

If you want to be sort of fancy

> Make a glaze by heating 2 c sugar, juice of one lime, and c water until it boils. Allow to cool for just a minute and add 1/4 c tequila and 2 tbsp Grand Marnier. (If you have done a good job of taste-testing the tequila, the label may read "Grand Mariner.") Pour over the cakes while they are still warm. They will still qualify as teacakes because the glaze is invisible when it soaks in and dries.

If you want to be very fancy (and change the name to cupcakes)

> Make a white icing with 4 c confectioner's sugar, 1 c shortening, 2 tbsp water, 1 tbsp Grand Marnier (or Mariner). If it is too thick to spread, add more liqueur! Just mix all this together for five minutes. Top with lime zest for prettiness.

If you want to be downright decadent

> Glaze, then frost too!

Christine Russell

Parallax View
Jim McGarrah

Tonight, I drink enough tequila
that when I change barstools
without falling, the barmaid laughs.
She knows my short trip home
will bring applause from neighbors
who wonder what new existential
crisis drove me into this stupor.
I will entertain, but not confess,
the notion that my silence
protects them all from wisdom,
a thing so profound its existence
shifts perspective in direct proportion
to agave consumption. For example,
I am certain that the Cuervo bottle
has climbed upward from bottom
to top shelf after several shots
and nestles now next to Gran Patron.
Is it a taste thing? No. It's a miracle,
like Nietzsche resurrected as Jesus,
like discovering the car next to mine
isn't the one moving as I drive away.
Suffering these revelations that might be
called "parallax views" as others do arthritis
brings me relief from the soreness
of bone rubbing bone in my brain
during what uninformed people call life.

Uncovering the Mystery of Mezcal
Michele Ostrove

Para todo mal mezcal y para toda bien tambien
—Popular proverb ("As a remedy for everything bad, mezcal, and
to celebrate all good as well")

Like Scotch or Champagne, mezcal is one of those spirits whose taste
speaks volumes about its place of origin. Each sip reflects the layers of
flavor of Oaxaca, the most topographically varied state in Mexico; its
indigenous Indian population; time-honored traditions; and prized agave
plant.

It all starts with what the French call *terroir*, the subtle differences in
soil composition and the local growing season, which are key to the quality
of agave, also known as maguey. Only about a quarter of the 50 varieties
of maguey that grow in Oaxaca are used for mezcal, but it is chiefly made
from the *espadín* agave, a relative of the tequila-yielding blue agave. The
plants take root from runners in small plots in villagers' gardens for about
two years, and then are uprooted and transported to the outlying hills to
grow until they reach maturity—a process that can take up to a decade. In
accordance with biodynamic and organic farming methods, the agave is
often harvested during the new moon, which is believed by the Zapotec to
have a profound influence on its flavor. Its long, sharp leaves are removed,
and the *piñas* (named for the pineapple appearance of their bodies) are
split by hand using an ax. And that is only the beginning of the laborious,
tradition-guided process of distillation.

The *piñas* are placed on red-hot rocks in a *palenque* (large, conical
pit), where logs of *encino*, a local black oak, have been left smoldering for
a few days. They are then covered with various materials, such as fiber
from the agave plant, banana leaves or woven palm-fiber mats, and sealed
airtight by a layer of earth. Three to five days later, the smoky *piñas* have
begun the process of fermentation and are ready to be crushed. Crushing
is most often accomplished with the help of horsepower—by a large,
circular millstone pulled by horse—but in a few places, the *maguey* is
ground by men wielding oak bats.

The crushed *maguey* is rinsed, made into a *tepache* (mash) using a
little water, and placed in fermentation vats. There, its wild yeasts are left
to mingle with the microbes that are specific to each village's altitude.

Once fully fermented, the agave is put through a wood-fired distillation process, concentrating the alcohol and separating the impurities. This leaves the *corazón*, or heart of the distillate. Depending on the type of mezcal, the *mezcalero* may put the liquid through several distillations to soften its intensity and refine its flavor.

One of the most unique and rare mezcals is *pechuga* (breast), named after its key ingredient, a raw, skinless chicken breast. Individualized by closely guarded family recipes, *Pechuga* is made once a year by redistilling the finished mezcal with a mix of seasonal fruits, such as plums, apples, bananas, quince, pineapple and guava. A chicken breast hangs from the cap of the still and is quickly cooked by the steam, dripping tiny bits of protein and fats that give the mezcal a subtle flavor nuance. Although *Pechuga* is generally produced in small amounts for personal consumption, it is exported to the United States by a couple of distributors, including the Taos, New Mexico-based distributor Del Maguey, on a first-come, first-served basis. Among the exclusive venues worldwide that serve *Pechuga* are the Big Star restaurant in Chicago and the Agave Lounge in Santa Fe, New Mexico's Eldorado Hotel.

Like other exquisite spirits worldwide, *Pechuga* carries a hefty price tag (about $200 a bottle), but agave aficionados consider it more than worth it.

The Smoky Margarita
courtesy of Agave Lounge at the Eldorado Hotel & Spa in Santa Fe

1.5 oz. Partida Reposado Tequila
0.5 oz. Del Maguey Mezcal
1 oz. Agave Syrup
1 oz. Fresh Pressed Lime

Shake and strain over fresh ice with a salted rim garnished with a lime wheel.

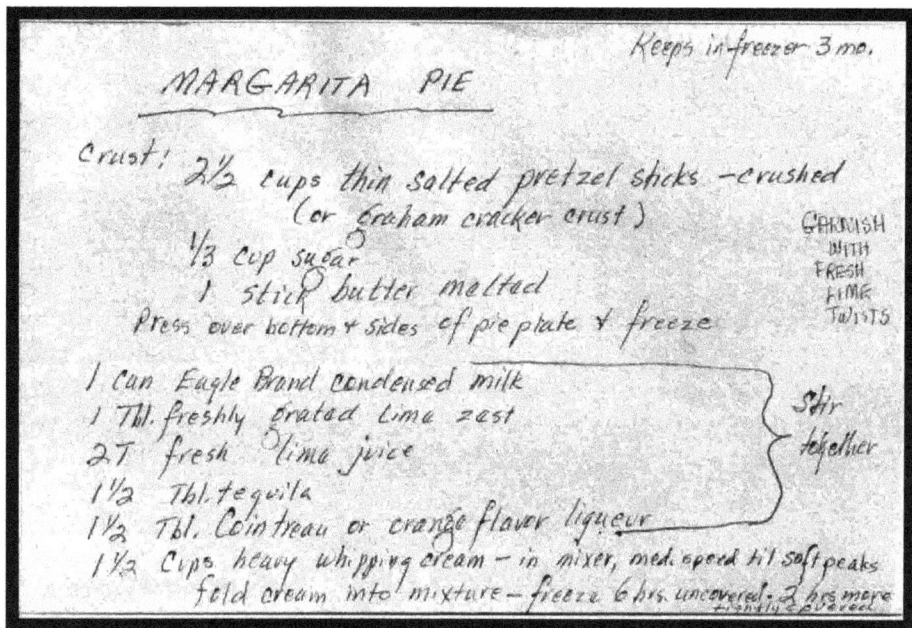

MARGARITA PIE

Keeps in freezer 3 mo.

Crust: 2½ cups thin salted pretzel sticks —crushed
(or graham cracker crust)
⅓ cup sugar
1 stick butter melted
Press over bottom + sides of pie plate + freeze

GARNISH WITH FRESH LIME TWISTS

1 can Eagle Brand condensed milk
1 Tbl. freshly grated lime zest
2 T fresh lime juice
1½ Tbl. tequila
1½ Tbl. Cointreau or orange flavor liqueur

Stir together

1½ Cups heavy whipping cream — in mixer, med. speed til soft peaks
fold cream into mixture — freeze 6 hrs. uncovered, 3 hrs more lightly covered

A Mother of Invention
a recipe from Norma Brown, with a few words from her son

So, what's a Baptist preacher's wife to do when her son develops a taste for tequila and margaritas?

To begin with, she searches through old editions of *Southern Living* from the 70s for recipes that might help her to "do a little something for him" now and then. She finds one. It's for Margarita Pie. What good Baptist could be faulted for making a pie—even if tequila is a main ingredient? Then she recruits her beloved older brother, who's a Methodist down in Texas, to buy a cheap bottle and sneak it to her on a late-night run up I-35 some weekend. Finally, with this most difficult and illicit step taken care of, she goes to work on the graham cracker crust, which—in spite of God's strict commandments against gluttony—has enough butter in it to kill a small horse and yet is, for some reason, perfectly... and theologically... acceptable.

As for concerned church members, who are hearing rumors... what can she say, besides maybe, "My son's love for the fermented things in life is a genetic predisposition, not a 'choice.' We love and support him for who he is. And we always will."

The Middle Name of Evil
Alan Birkelbach

The word Evil is so over-used. Skeletor is Evil. I don't think I'll get any debate on that. But He-Man really needs Skeletor else he's kind of purpose-less, so any Evil that exists just so Good can look better and more muscular might not really be Evil after all. Hmm. I'll have to think a while on that.

I'm already digressing and I've barely gotten started. The first time I faced tequila. Of course, that isn't the best title for this campaign, is it? Any time submissions are requested from multiple authors for some type of thematic book there are entries you just know you are going to get: some will be very well constructed poetic pieces built around some vaguely autobiographical event. Some will be based on some other well-known piece, poetic or otherwise, maybe some satiric, but cute, takeoff on Spenser or Yeats or Dr. Seuss, lines almost lifted but not quite. You can depend on some entries that will decry against whatever the main theme is (maybe a weepy story about a tragic car accident—there always has to be an entry about a car accident—it's the unspoken submission law). Some entries will be scholarly, some very contrived—and then some will be flatout bad. And of those bad ones you still have to take and publish some percentage of those because of space or political or he-bought-me-a-beer-once issues.

And besides, writing an entry, be it poetic, essay, fiction, or creative non-fiction, on any specific theme is beyond some people's reach. They can't do it. It's like telling them to write an occasional poem. "Quick. Uncle Alvin may die in the next two days and we need someone to write something really nice and poetic about him. Make it rhyme. Mention his cufflink collection. And how he liked beans." Yeah, yeah. Even better. Tell one of those writers they have ten minutes to practice because by god they're next in line to sing the National Anthem at the World Series. Performance on demand. Some minds are not suited for it.

So, it's a tough confession but there it is. I hadn't ever experienced that embarrassing euphoria aptly entitled 'Being Drunk' before and I happened, there in my first semester at college, to mention it to a girl I was trying to impress. Your parents don't teach you the concept of performance on demand. Well, some of them do. If you're in Select Soccer and you're, like ten years old and still trying to work out the whole looking-cool-while-running thing (today I'll try short strides because when I tried pointing my toes yesterday I just looked like ballet-girl) and your folks are saying 'Perform! Do your Best!' and that whole 'best' thing seems pretty finite and you're only ten FOR CRYING OUT LOUD and, well, some kids are still waiting for brilliance to catch them in perfect running stride.

One of the things about Evil is that you probably shouldn't say its name. Fat women say that chocolate is Evil. Let me visually imagine fat women and chocolate together. Yup. They're probably right. But E-V-I-L (maybe if I spell it it's not as potent) has a lot of talents and I'm thinking one of them is the way it can personalize itself, make itself unique to the situation or person. Aboard the Nautilus the giant Octopus had to go for Kirk Douglas. Ultimately the swordfight had to go down to Luke and Darth—or Errol and Basil. That, um, Darkness, was best suited for those Heroes. Had to be that way. Of course, part of what has to be considered here is the seductive nature of Evil. Get the connection? It's like an on-line dating service.

Oh, we could have that discussion here, couldn't we? The whole 'some things are Fated or meant by Blood-lines to happen' versus the 'existential let's see how it comes out' view. Not like we get to fill out a questionnaire, like EVER. No. Back to the on-line dating. You get all these questions. It's like you're trying to plan out Fate, wanting to skip the bad dental jobs and highmaintenance stalkers and go directly to the good stuff. Buddy, I gotta tell ya—on-line dating is proof that Fate does exist and using one of those services is like buying an electric hammer—you get there faster but you're not sure it was worth paying for.

So, this girl, whose name I will not mention because she made it a very clear point to drop out of my life later after seeing the enormity of my naiveté, seemed to be knowledgeable about the best route to experience a drunken state—and she mentioned two words: Tequila Sunrise. (Later, in recovery phase, that was stretched out to five words. The Big E and Time seem to work hand in hand. It is an illusion but when you are in the middle of an event, trust me, Time does all kinds of strange things. A syllable can take forever to say.)

I drove and she told me what to buy. Sunrise. What a beautiful word. How could anything with such a beautiful word be a bad thing? It had connotations of flowers and dew and birds singing and ah, the scent of fresh-cut hay, waking up with the woman of your dreams nestled on your arm (and not having to be concerned about the coyote-limb-in-the-trap thing). Yes. A Tequila Sunrise. It seemed so pleasant, so smooth a route to a happy stupor.

There are some things you just know—and some things you just don't. There are some things you see happening; they don't seem to be immediate portents, but later you realize they had doom written in capital letters all over them. DOOM, DOOM, DOOM. Like Jungle drums. The key word here wasn't Sunrise. It was Tequila.

There are points in some stories where, if you look back, you just know Tequila was involved. When Eli Wallach has just taken the pistol from Yul Brynner (and the rest of the magnificent seven), and Eli is sitting there drinking, you just know it's tequila he's drinking (while Yul is standing there looking dark and angry and sober). Right there, man, right there, you know Eli is doomed. Tequila carries doom with it. Whoever trusts it is doomed too. And here's another one. When Liberty Valance is stumbling down the street, intent on killing Rance, and Liberty is crazy drunk but still a great shot, and you just know he's going to kill Rance, it's so inevitable. Liberty is drunk on whiskey. No tequila is involved right? Events should just play out and the good guy will die. But no. And it took me years to understand this. It's again one of those things you have to learn later, the role that the Big E plays in the invisible background. We're never told this but I'm sure Liberty Valance's middle name is—Tequila. Just look at how the movie comes out. Liberty was DOOMED, DOOMED, DOOMED from the get-go. Yeah. You just watch the whole movie. You'll understand it now.

That first Tequila Sunrise allowed me to carry a life preserver, a map that illustrated the back-out clause. I could still walk away. But after that second one it was like meeting the troll at the bridge who makes you answer three questions. It's when you get to the American or European swallow question that suddenly you realize baby you're committed to the path. Nothing you've read up to this point has prepared you for this. Dylan Thomas didn't drink tequila. Obviously. Tequila does not carry you gentle into a good night, true. It actually denies that you're drunk, that you're dying, and that night even exists. Hemingway drink tequila? Probably not. Agave doesn't grow on Kilimanjaro. Although I do believe he would have discovered a whole new meaning about the clanging of the bell tolling. After too many sunrises anything that makes a sound is a bell tolling. But I get ahead of myself.

When you're young you think you're Samson, long hair, indestructible, looking good without a shirt. You can stick your hands in a lion's carcass and pull out honey for crying out loud. But you go to one party, just one, and you drink too much, and you wake up all baldy-looking and the official news reports say it was wine and actually I would tend to agree because whew, man, if you had been drinking tequila you would have woken up with a kick-me tattoo and a full Brazilian and there would never have been the push on the pillars bring the temple down scene. You still got to be the hero.

After three Tequila Sunrises, (did I mention they were made in an ice-tea glass?), you feel like the guy in Momento who's constantly disoriented and having to introduce himself. It isn't so much that the brain gets unwrinkled. It's more like you have signed up, voluntarily, for the Zombie Army. Somebody talked you into it. Consider that there is a special circle of Hell where Dante talks about drunks. Well, he would not have mentioned Tequila over-usage specifically (metrically I'm not sure the word Tequila should be woven into any fixed form) and I'm pretty darn certain he didn't have a slot or room or rocky shelf reserved for Zombies—but after three sunrises you realize that this was Dante's big omission. There should be a special circle of Hell for Tequila. It is its own type of, well, Evil. (Here I will say it out loud. In this context I'm not calling it—just describing. Noun, adjective—big difference.)

Even Dante had a Virgil, a leader through the various circles. Virgil was his back-out clause—but only because there was no circle of Tequila. If there had been then the whole story would have just stopped, lines incomplete, no two more interminable and less interesting parts. Jammed up right there like Coleridge's Xanadu. (And while I bring that Coleridge moment up I have to say it's another of those instances like the Liberty Valance situation where Tequila played an insidious invisible role. Yes, Coleridge had taken something, maybe absinthe, maybe opium, and yes, he did wake up with an exquisite vision and began writing the jewel of a poem Kubla Khan— until he was interrupted by a knock on his door, a mysterious 'person from Porlock'. We have never been given more information about that person but I can tell you that level of malevolent, writusinterruptus behavior can only have been performed by a Tequila Salesmen! It's the only answer, the only mind wormy and dark-veined enough to have kept us from the full glory of the pleasure domes.)

Going into the fourth sunrise there were no more pleasure domes. Zombies don't have pleasure domes. They have a guttural language. They lean against things. It's better if you shoot them in the head. That would have been better. Much better. When I was younger, no, I mean much younger, younger than that, my folks would say there are some things you should not talk about or see. Now we see them in commercials all the time. (The light beer commercials are funny, yes, but it's light beer and tasteless so I wish we wouldn't talk about it. And pizza commercials shown late at night after the pizza place has closed?! What's up with that? And dress commercials with women skinnier than anything I've ever dated (although maybe not as grateful) and me not having a date for at least six months and my Internet connection down? I don't need to see that either. Small Evil—but still Evil.)

But, as I said, the word Evil is overused. When you talk about Evil you should never completely describe it and never totally finish the story. There's always going to be Evil. Once Tequila was created, actually once that first agave seed was planted, a whole new and unique type of Evil was generated. Even if I could remember the rest of my story I have a literary and moral obligation not to recount it. If Evil is called on then it can be reanimated. I experienced my first drunk on tequila. I have been a zombie and come back. We will never speak of this again.

Apply Imagination
Carol Hamilton

Late afternoon, and the margaritas
are cheap, and all day cheap
at my nearby restaurant.
I think their tequila is applied
like fairy dust, a starry wand
wrist-flicked at the bulbous glass.
Lifting the slushy ice, the limey mix,
the chunky salt crystals, despite
everything, I magically
turn into a believer.

Tequila Nonsense
W.K. Stratton

No sotol on the shelf so I bought
A dusty fifth of tequila and drove
Toward Marathon, just one stop along
The way, the sky oozing purple
And red along the horizon until
Somewhere around Sanderson.
I found a place to park for the night
And broke the seal, the first fiery
Swallow dropping deep into my boots.
I leaned back against the stars and peeled
José Cuervo's name from the bottle,
Then drank more. I felt Jalisco
Swim through my blood and brooded:

If I had to do it over, I'd build a house
Of caliche, curse the rain, praise the wind,
And sing of los mesteños, ride like lightning –
Never fall to a woman, never own a credit card,
And proclaim: I refuse to bend to this age!
But then I reined myself:
Enough tequila nonsense.
I threw the bottle into
The dark-frustrated guajillos.

Down
Nathan Brown

A weekend in Vegas without gambling and drinking is just like being a born-again Christian.

—Artie Lange

At casino level, I walked by in awe of the tourist's ability to stand on bad shoes in collar-pullingly long lines for Expensive Tickets to see Cheap Trick... or... a chance to overeat at a buffet where none of us will know when to walk away from the table any better than we do from Blackjack or the hypnotic spin of the Roulette wheel.

Anyway, these lines drove us—being the misanthropes we are—down the boulevard to the low-rent district of Excalibur and the Luxor where, for instance, the lobby of New York New York felt like a Disneyland-scale sports bar—a thing ten-times as terrifying, at least to me, as Freddy Krueger ever dreamed of being in yet another bad sequel.

We walked back out the doors of the MGM Grand the moment we walked in and saw a glowing movie-poster-sized sign for Starbucks with a big green arrow pointing off into the growing darkness—just one of many possible gateways to hell in this town.

But it's not as if any hotel in Vegas is much more than a theme-airport with a nice yet thin veneer and a good number of slot machines.

However, I feel it only fair to mention that the end of our particular line brought us to Mandalay Bay where we finally felt weak enough to have to eat something. And this is when we happened onto Hussong's. Their wild mushroom version of Queso Fundido caught our attention on the menu. But let's be honest here, any place with big letters on its sign that read:

LESS ICE
MORE TEQUILA

I mean, c'mon...

Besides, I'm a great appreciator of restaurants that include an educational element along with their culinary offerings.

I know it seems a guy with my special problem would already have some kind of grip on the history of the margarita. But I reveled in the news—however unreliable—that a bartender in the dust-choked border town of Ensenada created the drink for a beautiful woman... Margarita Henkel, the daughter of the German Ambassador to Mexico... back in October of 1941.

His name? Don Carlos Orozco. And in the history of civilization, so overrun with Huns, Khans, and Hitlers, he should be remembered as someone who fought to make the world a better place.

It matters not that some believe the woman was Rita Hayworth, whose given name was Margarita Carmen Cansino.

It matters only that Don Carlos imagined a better mix for the future...

a mix of tequila, Damiana, and lime over ice...

a future held in the humble vessel of a salt-rimmed glass.

[An excerpt from *Letters to the One-Armed Poet: A Memoir of Friendship, Loss, and Butternut Squash Ravioli*. Village Books Press, 2011]

CONTRIBUTORS

Alan Berecka and Annette Funicello were both born in Utica, New York. She went on to fame and fortune; he wrote a poem in which she appears and works a reference librarian at Del Mar College in Corpus Christi, Texas. His poetry has appeared in such places as American Literary Review, Texas Review, Ardent, Windhover, Christian Century, and *The Blue Rock Review*. His first full-length collection, *The Comic Flaw*, was published by neoNuma Arts in 2009. His second full collection, *Remembering the Body*, is forthcoming from Mongrel Empire Press.

Alan Birkelbach was the 2005 Poet Laureate of Texas. His work has appeared in journals and anthologies such as *Grasslands Review, Borderlands, The Langdon Review, and Concho River Review*. He has 6 books in prints and 2 more scheduled for 2011. He swore off tequila in the 70's and only occasionally goes back to prove he still hates it.

Jerry Bradley is Professor of English at Lamar University. He is the author of five books including *The Movement: British Poets of the 1950s* (Twayne), *Simple Versions of Disaster* (University of North Texas Press), which was commended by the *Dictionary of Literary Biography*, and most recently *The Importance of Elsewhere* (Ink Brush Press). A member of the Texas Institute of Letters, Bradley was chosen as the 2000 Joe D. Thomas Scholar-Teacher of the Year by the Texas College English Association, and he received the 2005 Frances Hernandez Teacher-Scholar Award by the Conference of College Teachers of English. His poetry has appeared in many literary magazines including *New England Review, American Literary Review, Modern Poetry Studies, Poetry Magazine*, and *Southern Humanities Review*. He is also poetry editor of *Concho River Review*.

Milton Brasher-Cunningham has worked as a pastor, youth minister, hospital chaplain, chef, and high school English teacher—and those are just the full time jobs. He lives in Durham, North Carolina with his wife and three Schnauzers and spends much of his free time chasing food trucks and listening to the Boston Red Sox on the radio. He writes (almost) daily at www.donteatalone.com and is always willing to meet for margaritas.

Ashley Brown is a teacher and tutor in Norman, Oklahoma. Originally from Houston, she taught English at Episcopal High School for many years, worked in the music business as an agent, and did freelance editing. She currently teaches at the University of Oklahoma; serves as the director of Tutor and Test Prep; tutors students in writing, study skills, and ACT prep; and continues to freelance edit, as well as work to perfect her margarita mixing skills.

Nathan Brown is a musician, photographer and award-winning poet from Norman, Oklahoma. He holds a PhD from the University of Oklahoma and teaches there as well. Mostly though, he travels now, performing readings and concerts, as well as leading workshops and speaking in high schools, universities, libraries, and community organizations on creativity, creative writing, and the need for readers to not give up on poetry. He has published seven books—*Letters to the One-Armed Poet: A Memoir of Friendship, Loss, and Butternut Squash Ravioli,* just came out this spring, and a previous book, *Two Tables Over,* won the 2009 Oklahoma Book Award. His poem, "Little Jerusalems," just received a Pushcart Prize nomination. Nathan has also recorded several albums of all original songs. His newest CD, *Gypsy Moon,* was released in the spring of 2010.

Norma Brown has a degree in education and art from Oklahoma Baptist University. For over two decades, she taught both private and group classes, led workshops, and held one-artist shows in impressionistic oils. She continues to paint commissions for clients of favorite locales or their children in landscape. She has won numerous awards locally and nationally. She was recently juried into Oil Painters of America.

Julie Chappell learned to drink tequila, not in Texas, but in Seattle where drinking tequila was a required skill honed in a wild landscape where winter nights were long and summers short. Along with her lessons in Margarita rocks, slammers, and salt and lime balance, she earned her Ph.D. at the University of Washington. She is now Associate Professor of English at Tarleton State University where she teaches creative writing, Shakespeare, and other early literature with salt and lime perfectly balanced.

Lisa Craig is a marketing project manager for a national home builder. She has served as art editor for several journals and has won awards for her photography and newspaper writing.

Sherry Craven has called both West Texas and East Texas home for much of her life. She has taught college English, creative writing, and high school Spanish. Recently, she retired and now lives in Jasper, Deep East Texas. She has published poetry, short fiction, and creative nonfiction and read poetry for NPR. Her poetry has appeared in English and Spanish in journals such as *Amarillo Bay, Muse2, New Texas, Two Southwests, The Witness, Windhover, descant, The Langdon Review, RiverSedge, The Texas Review, Concho River Review, El Locofoco*, and she has essays in the anthology *Quotable Texas Women*. Her poetry appears in the anthology of *Texas writers Texas Poetry 2*, and her nonfiction in *Writing on the Wind*, a collection of essays by West Texas women writers. Her new book of poetry, *Standing by the Window*, was published by Virtual Artists Collective in 2010.

Terry Dalrymple's publications include *Fishing for Trouble*, a novel for middle readers, *Salvation*, a collection of short fiction, and *Texas Soundtrack*, a book of stories he edited. He serves as fiction editor for *Concho River Review* and is a member of the Texas Institute of Letters. He teaches English at Angelo State University.

Ebbesen Davis, an Austin-based artist, was born and raised in the farming communities of California's central valley. After moving to Texas in the mid seventies, he has worked in a wide variety of mediums, including photography. For over a dozen years he has been making stereo photographs, using both film and digital equipment. He often exhibits these by connecting them to supportive elements, using such diverse materials as wood, stone, copper tubing, and glass.

Daniella DeLaRue, writer and educator by training, photographer and garage mechanic by curiosity. She earned her B.A. and M.A. at Lamar University and is currently the Director of the McNair Scholars Program at Lamar University. Daniella has a lust for travel and a gastronomical inquisitiveness that she hopes she never satiates. She has also been known to jump out of perfectly good airplanes, which she will deny because there is no such thing as "a perfectly good airplane." By the way, she makes a mean agave margarita, but only if you ask her nicely.

Jeffrey DeLotto, Professor of English in the School of Arts and Letters at Texas Wesleyan University in Fort Worth, teaches writing, Shakespeare, and Modern British literature. A native of Florida, he has also taught writing and literature at Texas Tech University, at Yarmouk University (in Jordan), and as a Fulbright Lecturer in American Literature at the University of Plovdiv in Bulgaria. His poems, essays, and stories have appeared in numerous magazines, journals, and anthologies, and he has published a chapbook entitled *Voices at the Door*, the Southwest Poets Series winner from the Maverick Press, and *Days of a Chameleon: Collected Poems*. He also serves as General Editor for *Scholarship and Creativity On Line: A Journal of the Texas College English Association*, General Editor for Texas Wesleyan University Press, and Poetry Editor for the international on-line journal *AmarilloBay.org*.

Millard Dunn is Professor of English, Emeritus, at Indiana University Southeast, where he taught for 33 years. In 1983, his chapbook *Engraved on Air* won first prize in the Kentucky Arts Council Chapbook Contest. His other publications include *This Powerful Rhyme: A Workshop Approach to Shakespeare's Sonnets* (Co-authored with Ken Watson). His poetry has appeared in many literary magazines, among them *Concho River Review, Film and History, Kansas Quarterly, The Louisville Review, The Ohio Review, Poetry Northwest, Sandhills-St. Andrews Review, Shenandoah, Southern Poetry Review, Stand*, and *Tar River Poetry*. A collection of his poems, *Places We Could Never Find Alone*, is recently published by Inkbrush Press. He lives with his wife, Carole, in Louisville, Kentucky.

Andrew Geyer's books are *Siren Songs from the Heart of Austin* (Ink Brush Press 2010), *Dixie Fish* (Ink Brush Press, 2011), *Meeting the Dead* (UNMP 2007), and *Whispers in Dust and Bone* (TTUP 2003), which won the silver medal for short fiction in the *Foreword Magazine* Book of the Year Awards. Geyer's stories have appeared in numerous literary magazines and won many awards, including the Spur Award from the Western Writers of America for best work of short fiction published in 2003. A native Texan, Geyer currently lives and writes in Aiken where he serves as Assistant Professor of English at the University of South Carolina Aiken.

Gretchen Harries Graham is a mother, professor, curator, writer and fiber artist from the U.S. city of fountains, Kansas City, living in Austin, Texas. GHG is married to the Americana singersongwriter Jon Dee Graham. GHG loves jokes, laughing and Anejo.

Lyman Grant has taught at Austin Community College since 1978. Currently he serves as Dean of Arts and Humanities. He has published one chapbook and three volumes of poetry. The most recent book of poems is titled *As Long as We Need*. His poems have appeared in *Borderlands, Cider Press Review, Sulphur River Literary Review, Windhover, Concho River Review, descant,* and other journals.

Joyce Gullickson works as a Registered Nurse while pursuing her true vocation, Poetry.

Carol Hamilton is a former Poet Laureate of Oklahoma and has been nominated for a Pushcart Prize five times. She has won a Southwest Book Award, an Oklahoma Book Award, Cherubim Award, *Chiron Review* Chapbook Award, David Ray Poetry Prize, the Byline Literary Awards for both short story and poetry, and the Warren Keith Poetry Prize. She is a former elementary school teacher, college and university professor who is currently a volunteer translator at Variety Health Clinic.

Gary Hawkins writes poems; writes on Modern and contemporary poetry; and writes and presents on the scholarship of teaching and learning. This work has appeared in *Virginia Quarterly Review, born magazine, Emily Dickinson Journal,* and *Teaching Creative Writing in Higher Education*. He lives in Black Mountain, North Carolina, where he teaches in the Undergraduate Writing Program and is Associate Dean at Warren Wilson College, an historic work college where students form the campus workforce—and he spends part of each summer in Addison County, Vermont.

A. William Hinson lives in San Leanna, Texas with his wife Elizabeth, granddaughter Destiny and Deuce the dog. After retiring from government service, much of it spent overseas, he spends his time writing songs, building gadgets, and collecting movies.

James Hoggard, an award-winning author of twenty books and Poet Laureate of Texas for 2000, has had work recently in *Harvard Review, Southwest Review, Translation Review, The Dirty Goat,* and numerous others. His most recent collection of translations of poems by Oscar Hahn (Chile, 1938), *Ashes In Love*, was named by Poetry International as one of the "notable books" published in 2008 and 2009.

R Dean Johnson's essays and stories have appeared in, among others, *Juked, Natural Bridge, New Orleans Review, Slice*, and *The Southern Review*. He is an Assistant Professor at Eastern Kentucky University and a member of the core faculty in the Bluegrass Writers Studio. He lives in Richmond, KY with his wife, the writer Julie Hensley, who makes fun of him for liking Strawberry Margaritas.

Cindy Jordan—In 1983, every country radio station and honky-tonk was playing, "José Cuervo you are a friend of mine." This is the first song Cindy Jordan ever wrote. The song "José Cuervo" went on to be the 1983 Country Music Song of the Year in *Billboard Magazine*. Since then Cindy has written several genres of music. She is a speaker, entertainer, composer and author. Her book, *Butterfly Moments*, tells the story of how Tequila started her on the path of enlightenment. Visit her at cynthiamusic.com. She'd love to hear from you.

Robert Ashker Kraft received a Bachelor's Degree from the University of Texas at Austin, where he studied English Literature under the Plan II program. He was the recipient of the James A, Michner Undergraduate Fiction Scholarship. He has worked as an egg farmer, a private investigator, a cook, a fisherman, and many, many other things. He wrote and produced comedy pieces for Air America Radio. He currently operates VoiceKraft Audio in Austin, Texas, were he voices and produces audio for radio, TV, and film. He writes a blog called "Tales of the Factotum." He sings with The Robert Kraft Trio at various venues around Austin and Texas.

Lise Liddell earned her Bachelor of Science in Liberal Arts in 1985, and her Masters in Business Administration in 1987 from the University of Texas at Austin. After a short stint in the business world, she took an early retirement to begin acting, singing, and writing songs. She has released three musical CD's: *White Heart, Lovers' Moon*, and *In the Wake*. Her fourth CD, *Laced*, was released in the spring of 2011. Ms. Liddell lives in Houston, Texas, enjoys traveling, studying psychology, reading, and yoga.

Tony Mares says he was a poet born sometime in the late fifteenth century. He discovered tequila on one of the voyages with Columbus. Tequila has kept him still kicking around, still writing. His work includes *The Unicorn Poem & Flowers* and *Songs of Sorrow* (West End Press),

With the Eyes of a Raptor (Wings Press), and his translations of poems by the Spanish poet Ángel González, *Casi Toda la Música y otros poemas/Almost All the Music and Other Poems* (Wings Press), *Conversations I Never Had With Patrociño Barela*, (University of New Mexico Press). His most recent publication is a chapbook *Rio del Corazón*.

Anne McCrady's poetry, stories and essays appear internationally in a wide range of literary journals, magazines and anthologies. Her two poetry collections, *Along Greathouse Road* and *Under a Blameless Moon*, each won publication awards; many of her poems are also contest winners. A storyteller, inspirational speaker and workshop presenter, as well as an advocate for peace and community, Anne is the founder of InSpiritry, an effort to Put Words to Work for a Better World.

Jim McGarrah's poems, essays, and stories have appeared most recently in *After Shocks: Poems of Recovery, Avatar Review, Bayou Magazine, The Café Review, Connecticut Review, Elixir Magazine, Huntington Stone Review* and *North American Review*. His play, *Split Second Timing*, received a Kennedy Center ACTF Award in 2001. He is the author of two award-winning books of poetry, *Running the Voodoo Down* and *When the Stars Go Dark*, as well as a memoir of the Vietnam War entitled *A Temporary Sort of Peace*, which won the Eric Hoffer Legacy Non-Fiction Award in 2010 and the novel Going Postal. McGarrah has been nominated for three Pushcart Prizes and a finalist twice in the James Hearst Poetry Contest. He is editor, along with Tom Watson, of *Home Again: Essays and Memoirs from Indiana*. McGarrah's most recent nonfiction book, *The End of an Era*, was published by Ink Brush Press in the spring of 2011.

David Meischen has had poems in *The Southern Review, Southern Poetry Review, Borderlands, Cider Press Review*, and other journals, as well as *Two Southwests* (Virtual Artists Collective, 2008), which features poets from the southwest of China and the U.S. Meischen has participated in two collaborative shows—The Art in Fiber 2011 at the Copper Shade Tree in Round Top Texas and Threaded Lives: Poems from the Fiber World (Taos, NM, Rane Gallery, 2009). As a founder of Dos Gatos Press, he has served as co-editor for *Wingbeats: Exercises and Practice in Poetry*, a 2011 release. With a recent MFA in fiction writing, Meischen is working on a series of short stories set in fictional Nopalito, Texas. He has published two works of fiction.

Karla K. Morton, the 2010 Texas Poet Laureate, is a graduate of Texas A&M University, a member of the Texas Institute of Letters, and a Board Member of the Greater Denton Arts Council. A Betsy Colquitt Award Winner and an Indie National Book Award Winner, she has been widely published, and is the author of six books of poetry. She has been featured on television, radio (NPR) and newspapers across the US. A native Texan, Morton has recently discovered her love of Patrón and all things agave, and has trekked thousands of miles in her Little Town, Texas Tour, bringing poetry and the arts into schools, colleges, universities, civic groups, cancer support groups, and festivals in communities across her beloved state.

Antonia S. Murguia is a published poet whose writing keeps her young at heart. She celebrates poetry through her online business, Toni's Treasures, toni-treasures.com. She is a member of Alamo Area Poets of Texas, San Antonio Poets Association and Poetry Society of Texas. Antonia has won numerous poetry awards and is published in *Inkwell Echoes*, *Dreamcatcher*, and *Voices Across the River* anthologies. Her published books are *Walking In the Footsteps of Faith, He Comes for Us*, and *Whispers of Love*. Antonia enjoys designing graphic art, watercolor painting, gardening, theater, music, and traveling. She lives in San Antonio, Texas.

Laurence Musgrove is Professor and Head of the Department of English and Modern Languages at Angelo State University in San Angelo, Texas where he teaches courses in literature, composition, and creative writing. His most recent book is *Handmade Thinking: A Picture Book on Reading and Drawing*. More of Laurence's Tex cartoons can be found at www.cartoonranch.com.

Patrick Ocampo was born in Manila in the Philippines and raised in Toronto Canada. He started his writing career in the first grade with a sci-fi epic about journeying to the moon with a dog. Since then he has published a collection of poems and short stories entitled *Surface Tension* and his work also appears in the Oklahoma anthology *Ain't Nobody Can Sing Like Me*. Patrick resides in Bartlesville, Oklahoma with his wife Christine Russell, four cats, and a dog who has no intention whatsoever of journeying to the moon.

Mary Ann O'Donnell has conducted ethnographic research in Shenzhen since 1995, photographing and creatively documenting the changing cityscape on the blog, Shenzhen Noted.

Michele Ostrove is a food and travel writer and president of the New Mexico-based Wings Media Network, a PR and marketing firm specializing in the hospitality industry. She was founder of *Wine Adventure*, the first wine magazine for women. Most recently, she organized New Mexico Restaurant Week and the Santa Fe Harvest Festival.

David Parsons is the 2011 Poet Laureate of Texas. His third collection of poetry *Feathering Deep* is recently out from Texas Review Press. His first book *Editing Sky* was winner of the Texas Review Poetry Prize and a Violet Crown Book Award Special Citation. He is a recipient of an NEH Dante Fellowship to SUNY, the French/American Legation Poetry Prize, and descant's Baskerville Publishers Poetry Prize. Parsons teaches Creative Writing and Racquetball/Handball at Lone Star College-Montgomery. He was inducted into The Texas Institute of Letters in 2009. His website is www.daveparsonspoetry.com

Juan Manuel Perez, a Mexican-American poet from La Pryor, Texas, is the author of *Another Menudo Sunday* (2007), the e-book *O' Dark Heaven: A Response To Suzette Haden Elgin's Definition Of Horror* (2009), and the new book *WUI: Written Under The Influence Of Trinidad Sanchez, Jr.* (2011), as a well as, six poetry chapbooks, including the acclaimed *Dial H For Horror* (2006). Juan is also the 2011-2012 Poet Laureate for the San Antonio Poets Association.

Yang Qian is the Artistic Director and founder of Fat Bird Theatre, Shenzhen. Most recently, Fat Bird premiered *Eye of the Universe*, a sci-fi musical and collaborated with SZCat to create "One Cat Six Days" for the First Shenzhen Fringe Festival.

James Ragan is the author of *In the Talking Hours, Womb-Weary, The Hunger Wall, Lusions, Selected Poems, The World Shouldering I, Too Long a Solitude*, and co-editor of *Yevgeny Yevtushenko: Collected Poems*. His plays include *The Landlord, Saints*, and *Commedia*. Translated into a dozen languages, he has been honored with three Fulbright Professorships, two Honorary Doctorates, the Emerson Poetry Prize, nine Pushcart

Prize nominations, a Poetry Society of America Citation, and the Swan Foundation Humanitarian Award. He has read for five heads of state including Mikhail Gorbachev and Vaclav Klaus, and his poetry has been recorded at Carnegie Hall, and for Sony and Rhino Records. He has a Ph.D. in English and for 25 years directed the Graduate Professional Writing Program at the University of Southern California.

David Rains alternates time between Houston and San Diego, oscillating between business development work for the software industry and advocacy for craft beer and spirits. His Ph.D. in music composition from the University of Texas provides an oblique touchstone for his opinions and a possible explanation for his eccentricities. (His personal margarita recipe includes marinating lime zest in its own juice for several hours.)

Hannah Rappaport is completing a memoir of when her spirit was taken from a suburban housewife life with two children to and through an ancient Gnostic initiation. For ten years, with the help of a Hungarian Gnostic Bishop and a Norwegian artist priest, she forged through the ritual sacraments of mystical Christianity (she was born in Israel, a Jewess). After she was ordained to the priesthood she left the church and continued learning wisdom in a wider arena. She lives and writes in Taos, New Mexico.

Beth Robinson lives in Oklahoma City. Her favorite quote is by Dr. Martin Luther King, Jr., "Darkness cannot drive out darkness; only light can do that..."

Christine Russell is a scientist by trade and an artist at heart. Photography is in her blood, a passion handed down by her grandmother. She lives in Oklahoma with one husband, one dog, and four cats.

Kellie Salome lives in Austin, Texas and attends St. Edward's University, where she is studying for her degree in Creative Writing. She is the recipient of the 2011 Scott Scribe Scholarship from The Writer's League of Texas, the winner of the Southwest Pop Culture 2010 Jerry Bradley Award for Creative Writing and and the 2009 Undergraduate winner of the TACWT Award for Creative Non-Fiction. She earns a living bartending at the world famous Continental Club. She makes very good margaritas. Mmmm...margaritas...

Barrie Scardino is an architectural writer who has published numerous articles and lectured onTexas architecture. She is former managing editor of *Cite Magazine: The Architecture and Design Review* of Houston and has co-authored three books on architecture: *Houston's Forgotten Heritage* (1991, Rice University Press); *Clayton'sGalveston* (2000, Texas A&M University Press) and *Ephemeral City* (2003, University of Texas Press). She also works asan editorial consultant and freelance writer for various other projects, including a cookbook. She adds tequila to everything.

Steven Schroeder is the co-founder, with composer Clarice Assad, of theVirtual Artists Collective (a "virtual" gathering of musicians, poets, and visual artists, vacpoetry.org). His most recent collection (with Debby Sou Vai Keng) is *a guest giving way like ice melting: thirteen ways of looking at laozi.*

Audell Shelburne is an Associate Professor of English and Chair of the Department of Languages and Literature at Northeastern State University in Tahlequah, Oklahoma. He is an assistant textual editor for *The Variorum Edition of the Poetry of John Donne*, working specifically with the texts of the verse letters. He has published poems in *descant, Borderlands*, and a number of smaller venues. He is currently revising a set of poems about life in the desert for a book-length manuscript, tentatively titled *Water from Rocks*.

Sandra Soli, Oklahoma poet and photographer, enjoys collaborative projects with artists in other disciplines. She admires all things beautiful, including the way grenadine drifts its rosy way through liquids, deceiving those who think nothing dangerous is happening.

Jim Spurr is a retired insurance adjuster and a nationally published poet since 1993. He's a graduate of Oklahoma Baptist University and one of two hosts at a monthly open mic in Shawnee, Oklahoma. His wife, Aline, is a Sr. VP at Arvest Bank.

Melvin Sterne went to a party when he was fifteen and came home when he was thirty-five. The party was in El Paso, and they drink a little tequila there. Melvin once dropped and broke a full bottle of Cuervo, still wrapped in the brown-paper liquor store bag, and gulped the tequila (broken glass and all) until the bag disintegrated. Somehow or another, he survived.

Today he directsdirects the Passport to Excellence Program and teaches Business Communications at the S P Jain Center of Management in Singapore. He has published 20 short stories in magazines of national and international circulation (with several winning awards), in addition to the occasional essay and poem. His first novel, *Zara*, is forthcoming from Ink Brush Press. "The Number You Have Reached" was originally published in *storySouth*. You can read more about him and his writing at www.melvinsterne.com.

W.K. Stratton's collection of poems, *Dreaming Sam Peckinpah*, was published in September 2011 by Ink Brush Press; his next book, *Floyd Patterson*, will be published by Houghton Mifflin Harcourt in the summer of 2012. Earlier works by W.K. Stratton (Kip) include *Backyard Brawl*, *Chasing the Rodeo*, and *Boxing Shadows*.

Larry D. Thomas, a member of the Texas Institute of Letters, was the 2008 Texas Poet Laureate. He has published sixteen collections of poetry, most recently *A Murder of Crows* (Virtual Artists Collective 2011). He enjoys listening to Beethoven, visiting art museums, and spending time with his wife, Lisa, and two Long-haired Chihuahuas, Pecos and Piñon.

George Wallace is an adjunct professor of literature and writing at Pace University in Manhattan and is author of twenty-one chapbooks of poetry. In addition to regular appearances in the New York area he travels internationally to conduct poetry workshops and read his work. In 2011 he was named Writer In Residence at the Walt Whitman Birthplace in New York.

Robert Whitsitt has published the online quarterly literary magazine *Amarillo Bay* (amarillobay.org) since 1999. He has been a high school math teacher in Pennsylvania; a service station attendant in Illinois and California; an office worker and programmer at Chevron; a technical writer for Texas Instruments and various Texas, California, New York, Oregon, Wisconsin, and Washington companies; a Web site designer, writer, and producer; and a software quality assurance engineer in Texas and California, most recently at Google.

Scott Wiggerman is the author of two books of poetry, *Presence*, new from Pecan Grove Press, and *Vegetables and Other Relationships*. He is co-editor of *Wingbeats: Exercises and Practice in Poetry*; he is also co-founder of Dos Gatos Press, publisher of the annual *Texas Poetry Calendar*, now in its fourteenth year. His website is
http://swig.tripod.com

Robert Wynne earned his MFA in Creative Writing from Antioch University. A former co-editor of *Cider Press Review*, he has published 6 chapbooks, and 3 full-length books of poetry, the most recent being *Self-Portrait as Odysseus*, which was released this year from Tebot Bach Press. He's won numerous prizes, and his poetry has appeared in magazines and anthologies throughout North America. He lives in Burleson, TX with his wife and three rambunctious dogs. His online home is
www.rwynne.com.

www.ingramcontent.com/pod-product-compliance
Lightning Source LLC
Chambersburg PA
CBHW031845090426
42741CB00005B/360